# LIFE BEHIND THE CAMERA

## By Chuck Quinzio

ECKHARTZ
PRESS

I'd like to dedicate this book to everyone who has carried a camera in the great city of Chicago past and present. Although we compete, we are friends.

# A NOTE FROM THE AUTHOR

Everything that happened in this book is true, but some things might not be so true. They are true to my memory. Some names and places have been changed to protect the innocent (as well as the guilty).

*March 5, 1993*

I can still see the young Hispanic man with the gunshot wound to his chest, and I can still hear him struggling to breathe. I can hear the faint sound of gunfire and wailing police sirens in the distance; an unwanted Fourth of July atmosphere in this extremely violent part of Chicago.

I remember every detail vividly.

The kid fought harder and harder to breathe, and the sounds he was making got louder and louder. He was heavily tattooed, wore gang colors, couldn't have been more than a teenager, and was dying on the very streets that raised him. It struck me that there was no visible blood, just burn marks on his shirt outlining the hole in his chest cavity.

I had never experienced anything like this before, so my initial reaction was to get him some help, but as time passed, my safety—and the safety of the officers with me—became my main concern. We were in a dark alley. The shooter was still out there. The only illumination I had to videotape this kid's last moments came from the fluorescent glow of a streetlamp. He was moving his legs side to side, slowly losing his battle to stay alive.

One of the officers took off, heading toward a pitch-black gangway in the hope of finding the shooter. I stayed behind with his partner and the victim. The gunshots, although distant, were all around us, and I could tell it was starting to unnerve the hardened street-savvy officer with me.

"Shut off the fucking camera right now! Get low–get on your knees!"

My heart was beating through my chest. I was anxious,

waiting for the police backup that hadn't yet arrived. I just stood there, documenting a struggle for survival.

"Get down, Goddamn it!" The officer snapped. "Get low! Do you want to get your head blown off?"

I fell to a knee and lowered the camera. The kid's breathing got louder and louder. It was becoming obvious that it wouldn't be long before we attracted unwanted company, so the officer put his hand on the boy's throat.

"I'm not going to die because of a street piece of shit like you," he whispered. "The shooter is still out there, and we can't see him. Shut the fuck up. You're giving us away."

The young man's eyes began tearing, and it looked like he was coming to terms with his fate. He stopped blinking, and stared up to the darkened heavens. For a moment, he was quiet, but then he started breathing at a very rapid pace. The officer jumped to his feet, gun drawn, looking in different directions to make sure no one was coming our way.

Officer "Tough Guy" was scared shitless.

Reality was setting in for me too. Sirens that were once in the distance were now getting closer, but it wasn't much of a comfort yet. There was too much potential for any one of us to fall victim to a killer we might never see.

"Rick, don't shoot; it's me," cried the voice of the second officer. "I can't find the shooter."

My jumpy companion lowered his gun. The sirens were getting closer. The sound echoed off the garages that lined the alley. It gave us a newfound sense of hope that we would be all right, that our backup was finally arriving. The second officer made it over to us and knelt down. We both looked at the young man, who was now barely breathing at all. We watched his eyes as they danced back and forth, studying each one of us.

I looked for some sense of order in those fleeting moments. Should I put my obligation to my job first by covering the story, or should I focus on just surviving this chaotic situation? My career had always been about getting "that shot." "That shot" makes the story. "That shot" defines one's career.

But the dying man's eyes paralyzed me.

I didn't have the heart to put the camera in his face.

# Chapter

# THE NUNS, THE STONES, THE FUTURE

I was born in a rural Midwestern town with less than twenty thousand people. As someone blessed with nothing more than a limited amount of common sense and a healthy imagination, I took each day as it came. I armed myself with the only thing that made me acceptable to my peers and gave me comfort: the ability to laugh and to make others do the same.

Unfortunately, because I attended Catholic school, I was also taught at an early age that if you crossed paths with the unholy, you could be condemned to a life of eternal damnation. For a young boy, that was a lot to wrap your head around. If you disobeyed a rule or two or even stretched the truth, you could fry in hell. The nuns used that ticket to hell as their ace in the hole to keep me in constant check.

Their beady eyes would peer into my soul as I sat in my small wooden desk. I was steadfast in my mission to avoid eye contact with these penguin lookalikes, always wringing their hands and flashing their wedding rings, symbols displaying their marriage to God.

One day I witnessed one of them come up behind a friend of mine who was reading a book at his desk. She struck him on the side of the head with a blow so hard it knocked him out of the chair and onto the floor. My groggy and disoriented buddy took a few minutes to regain his composure and get settled back in his seat.

The class nicknamed this particular nun after the great Detroit Tigers southpaw pitcher Mickey Lolich. Sister Lolich was also a lefty with a lightning fast pick-off move. It always worked the same way. First, she would finish writing on the chalkboard. Next, she would set the chalk into the tray. She would then grab an eraser (the kind with the heavy plastic on one side), and– with a sneaky fast move any major league pitcher would envy– she would smack her target with pinpoint accuracy.

One day my friend Patrick, a previously convicted wise ass, was the intended target of the Lolich eraser of death. Sister Lolich had been monitoring his spitball-throwing antics and multiple obscene gestures all day and was just waiting for the right moment to pounce. Lolich knew the approximate distance of her intended target at all times.

But on this day and in this place she underestimated Patrick's cat-like reflexes. He followed her hand movements and picked up the flight of the eraser as it burst like a missile from the dark background of her vestments. Summoning all the concentration of Obi-Wan Kenobi, Patrick was now one with the projectile. At the last possible second, he shifted slightly to his left and successfully avoided the missile.

But it didn't exactly fall harmlessly to the ground. The high-speed eraser crashed into Karen Donnelly's nose instead. The impact was so great it shattered her cat-eyeglasses, snapped her body backward, rendered her limp, and left Karen face down on her blood-soaked book report on mold spores.

It was over. Sister Lolich had missed her target for the first time in her disturbingly sadistic teaching career.

We were stunned; the greatest of all time had missed her mark. But she didn't take defeat lightly. As she reluctantly helped Karen to the school nurse, Lolich offered nothing remotely close to an apology. Karen was openly sobbing, but not a smidgen of compassion came across Lolich's round wrinkled, weathered face.

Within an hour, Lolich evened the score by laying a cheap shot on Patrick; showing the entire class what Christian spirit was all about.

That night at the dinner table I told the story of Patrick's misfortune to my parents. My mother, slowly chewing her dinner, paused and answered me with a serious look.

"Sounds to me he had it coming," Mom said.

It was at that moment I realized I had no allies in the war against the nuns. Even my own parents feared these so-called messengers of God.

\* \* \* \* \*

President Kennedy had just been assassinated when the Beatles invaded America with their music and sense of fashion. I was one of God's soldiers. The Beatles or anyone like them were considered devils on earth to the nuns, yet *The Ed Sullivan Show* brought them into our living rooms on a Sunday night. After I witnessed their first American performance on our black and white Philco television set, I was blown away.

Evidently, the nuns watched the same thing that night in their nun lair because the next afternoon the class was ordered by our Christian overseers never to watch the Beatles again. They sent letters to all of our parents and ordered them to ban

*The Ed Sullivan Show* from our homes. The most exciting thing
I'd seen since I was old enough to realize I was condemned to
this small town was being taken away!

According to the nuns, rock and roll music brought the
evils of drugs and sex into the world. As I look back at it now,
I find it ironic that a group of forty and fifty-year-old women
preached so strongly against two things they never experienced.
But then one Friday, a miracle happened. The principal, the
oldest and nastiest nun of all of them, got on the school's public
address system and announced that she was sending home a
letter to our parents asking them to watch *The Ed Sullivan Show*
with us on the upcoming Sunday night.

According to her, the Beatles were making a return performance, and Sister wanted our parents to be proactive and
explain first-hand how negative these young men from England
were.

My classmates and I were elated. We cheered in our little
Catholic hearts and minds, until she pissed on our parade with
a final scary closing announcement.

"God's judgment is swift and final on those who sin or follow those who sin," she said.

Sunday night came, and my family and I huddled around
the television as we were instructed to do. My parents looked
nervous and unsure. Ed Sullivan opened the show, and you
could have heard a pin drop in my house. But the head nun
had gotten the wrong information. The musical guests were
from England, but they weren't the Beatles. Before we knew it,
Ed introduced the Rolling Stones, and my living room quickly
went from apprehension to sheer fear as Mick Jagger lunged toward the camera and sang an up-tempo version of "Let's Spend

The Night Together." The Stones were thugs, and they were singing about banging chicks on national television. I kept one eye was focused on my parents, while the other watched Jagger's spastic movements. He was shaking his hips and strutting around the stage. The women were going wild in the audience.

I remember one shot of Ed Sullivan wringing his hands and smiling off-stage. I glanced at my mother who was sitting in a dimly lit corner. She was obviously being consumed by fear. When the Stones ended their song, it was like a tornado had blown through my house. The television was shut off and not a word was spoken.

That's the night I realized there was an entire world out there. A world had been dropped right into my lap by television, showing me the awesome potential of the medium.

I also came to another conclusion. If the nuns were insinuating that listening to rock music would send me straight to hell, then those nuns could take their beliefs and kiss my grade school ass.

\* \* \* \* \*

Catholic school was a constant struggle for me. It demanded discipline I didn't have. As hard as I tried, I just never found my comfort zone with the system or the people who ran it. In fifth grade, the church recruited all the boys to become altar servers. This was something I had very little desire to do, but with some healthy prodding from friends and my mother, I signed up anyway.

We worked with Father Armstrong, who was an overweight, jolly kind of guy. Father was always polite around our parents, but a real prick to the altar servers. Today, if the good father was still around, he'd be the poster child for priest abuse. He even looked the part: bald up top with long hair on the sides, squinty shifty eyes, and terminal bad breath. But the thing that really shocked us about him was that Father Armstrong cursed when things didn't go his way.

When this servant of God would say "Shit" or even worse, "Goddamn it," it would stop me cold. I tried to subtly report this unsavory part of his personality to my mother, and again, I was greeted with a fair amount of skepticism.

"You must have misunderstood him," she replied. "Priests don't curse."

My altar-serving career came damn close to a screeching halt one Sunday morning when I wore gym shoes in church. When I put on my black and white vestments, I thought I looked sharp. My shoes were black and white, too. Everything matched. I walked out onto the altar to light the candles before mass started, genuflected, made the sign of the cross, and made eye contact with a buddy of mine in the front row, who discreetly gave me the finger. I lit the candles, genuflected again, headed into the back room, and was greeted with Father Armstrong's wrath.

"Who the fuck do you think you are?" he screamed. "Willis Reed? You don't wear gym shoes to serve mass. EVER!"

There was nothing I could say. He was parading around like a madman. The veins in his forehead looked like they were ready to burst. But this time was different. This outburst was in front of another altar server, who was equally stunned. This time his screaming voice was so loud that most of the people in the church heard him too.

On my walk home, I was confused. How can we put these people on a pedestal when they display behavior like that? As soon as I walked into my house, my mother greeted me. We had a few minutes of small talk, then she admitted she heard the whole thing.

"I'll stand by you," she said, "if you want to quit serving."

I wasn't sure what to do. Should I quit and surrender, or should I tough it out? I chose the latter. In a weird way, I'm glad I did, because by sticking with it, I gained exposure to some more of life's twists and turns.

Part of our duties as altar boys was to serve at weddings and funerals. The most moving thing I witnessed in my young life was watching a man who carried the casket of his newborn son from the hearse through the crowded church, up to the front of the altar. The boy was only a week old when he died. That father's strength and vulnerability mesmerized me. As he knelt in that church, with all eyes seemingly fixed on him, it looked as if he was watching part of himself being eulogized, as if he too was being buried. When the service was over, he thanked each one of the servers for our compassion and our time. I could barely acknowledge him. I had never before been confronted with death. It was when I began to understand how fleeting life could be.

*   *   *   *   *

I wasn't what you'd call an academic achiever. I'm pretty sure my family's phone number was the most frequently dialed number in the history of the school. Instead of paying attention to my instructors, I was partial to entertaining my neighbors.

The nuns told my parents that they were praying for me, twenty-four hours a day, seven days a week.

In retrospect, I think I had ADD or ADHD or another learning disability that hadn't been discovered yet. I wasn't a good student, and I didn't meet their expectations. After-school detention was my second home. Thanks to my big mouth, I got a lifetime of experience washing chalkboards and emptying trashcans. One day I felt tired of spending my after-school time confined to a classroom, so I confronted the nun who was watching after our small band of after-school delinquents.

"My mother is very pregnant, and my father is working late," I told her. "I really need to get home to be with Mom just in case the baby decides to make an early appearance."

This got her attention.

"Hurry home," she said, "and by all means, help your mother. Tell her my thoughts are with her. Go with God."

I immediately realized I should have played that card years sooner. Just like that I was freed from my captivity. Of course, the only problem with this story was that my mother was not pregnant, but nevertheless, it was a great scam! I had played the concerned son and had given the false illusion of being a good Christian servant at the same time. It was perfect!

The next day every nun in the school either smiled at me or said hello. The principal even patted me on the head and told me to have a great day. In class I followed my usual routine, but this time when I was laughing and joking, nothing happened. The teacher turned a blind eye. I had beaten the system. I was invincible. The girls smiled at me. The tough guys stood aside as I passed. I had found the kryptonite to bring them all to their knees. The nuns were helpless against my powers.

On the walk home, I smelled the flowers and the fresh cut grass. The birds were chirping a peaceful song on a perfect cloudless day, and I felt like a million bucks. When I got home, I sat happy and peaceful in front of the television set. It was sheer euphoria until my mother let out a shrill scream.

"Pete! Come here quick."

I'd never seen my father move so fast in my life. He ran into the living room.

"What does this mean?" he asked my mother. "What are they doing here?"

I peered around the corner and gingerly walked toward my parents. When I saw what they were looking at, I stopped cold.

"What have you done now?" my mother asked. "Why are they here?"

I couldn't breathe. A carful of nuns were slowly exiting like circus clowns exiting a mini clown car. There seemed to be an endless line of them coming up our drive, penguin lookalikes armed to the teeth with cakes, pies, and cookies. I felt light-headed, and my body went limp.

My once brilliant scheme was unraveling before my eyes. I needed an exit plan. My mother was red-faced and scared to death. She demanded an answer from me, something I had no intention of delivering, so I ran and hid in my room instead.

In a trembling voice my mother asked my father to answer the door. He declined.

"You wanted to send him to that school. This is your pay off."

From my room I heard the door open and a voice told my mother that all the nuns had baked something for her, figuring it would help her in her delicate state. When my mother opened the door further, she revealed my secret. She was not with child. Mom asked what they were talking about, and the black and white army explained. My mother screamed my name, but I was now under the bed. She yelled for me again. I tightened my grip on the shag carpet, cowering on the floor of my room.

"Forget it," I heard one of the nuns say. "He's a lost cause."

They took their baked goods with them, left the porch in a single file line, and wedged themselves back into their clown car.

I stayed under that bed for quite a while. I was expecting to be flushed out by my mother, but no one came for me. Eventually I decided to accept the consequences. I crawled out from under my hiding place and entered the living room. My mother and father were sitting on the couch.

My father got up and stepped toward me. Fearing a series of blows to the head and torso I froze, but the blows never came. He just passed by and gave me a half smile. My mother was ashen and lifeless. As I got closer, she turned her eyes to mine.

"You know you're killing me, don't you?"

"I know," I replied.

She slowly forged a smile. She understood me. Through all the trouble I caused her, she was a true mother. No matter what hell her child repeatedly rained down upon on her, she loved me.

* * * * *

On the final day of eighth grade, the principal announced a special going-away present for the graduating class. She introduced Mike Santarea, the school janitor and a long-time suspected illegal immigrant.

"Mike is going to serenade us with some traditional Mexican folk songs."

We were so stunned that he had more talents than cleaning up our vomit and urine that we gave him a stirring round of applause. He adjusted himself on a stool, and he let out a good size belch. Those of us lucky enough to have a front row seat on that Thursday morning were the first to notice the janitor was shit-faced. He also didn't speak a lick of English. We knew we were in for a hell of a show.

Mike started to strum his guitar. He played for about a minute, just strumming a peaceful little melody, and he wasn't half bad. Mike's guitar was a soundtrack to my thoughts as I scanned the room, looking at the faces of my classmates. These were the only friends I'd ever known. My thoughts drifted to the birthday parties, the sporting events, the laughter, and the tears. I was starting to feel sad that this would be the last time I'd ever see some of these people.

But then Mike started to sing.

He had his eyes closed, and words to what I assumed was a love song of some kind started pouring out of him. His voice was way off key, his movements were roughly the same as those of someone having a grand mal seizure, and the more he got into the groove, the worse he sounded. Not one soul in that room understood Spanish.

As he reached his big finish, Mike appeared to be either losing his motor skills or possibly going headlong into stroke mode. He was strumming the guitar with a vengeance and was heading for his big finale when he suddenly lifted his left butt cheek off the stool and cut a fart. As the room became saturated with the scent of refried beans, I gave one last parting glance to each of my classmates. No one returned the look.

I thought to myself, "What a fitting way to close out my Catholic school days."

# Chapter

# DAYS OF RADIO

I quickly adapted to the feeling of freedom you get in public high school. There were no nuns, no eyes following your every move. I do admit to hyperventilating in science class when they showed a documentary on penguins, but for the most part, I was over the fear. High school was the time you were supposed to get serious about your future and start laying the groundwork for college.

While most students even at that young age had some idea of what they wanted to do for a career, I spent my time fabricating a fake I.D.to buy beer for my friends and me. Class work just wasn't my forte. Again, I felt slowed down by ADD or ADHD, but an English teacher put it all into perspective for me. One day when I screwed up one of his tests, I got his diagnosis.

"You're mildly retarded," he said.

Although he was joking, I do remember thinking that maybe something was actually short circuited in my brain. Why didn't I have the drive or desire to become a doctor, lawyer, stockbroker, or banker? Hanging out was my pastime until I went with a friend to the local radio station one day. His mother sent him to give them some information about a charity event. It was a small station located above a Laundromat, and it wasn't too impressive from the street, but to me the inside was fascinating.

There were a bunch of different studios, mountains of records, albums, and 45s stacked everywhere, and I'll never forget that wonderful stereo-equipment smell. The sights and the smells of the place drew me in until another smell overpowered everything. That unmistakable cigar smell was coming from the back studio where the afternoon DJ was hosting his show. TC was his name, and playing Central Illinois favorite rock music was his game.

He had a full Afro, a handlebar mustache, a velvet shirt, cheap jeans, and a two-dollar cigar. I had witnessed the power of television and how it brought the world into your home, and now I was witnessing the inner workings of a radio station. I was intrigued.

The station manager introduced himself and said we could come back anytime to just hang out if we liked. My friend declined, but I jumped at the opportunity. As often as I could, I'd ride my bike to the station and just kill time. I became a fixture around there, and everyone went out of his or her way to be friendly. TC let me run the soundboard for him while he took phone calls from some of his small town groupies.

Horny housewives and strippers from a nearby men's club were frequent visitors to the station, and TC used me as his buffer. I'd greet them in the reception area whenever a new one stopped by. I would entertain them while TC snuck a peek from another room. If they met his expectations, they got the studio tour, which usually ended with some form of sex act in the restroom. If they didn't pass the first glance test, I was the bearer of bad news, and they were asked to leave.

As time went on my duties increased. I was a gopher for

the DJs. My primary functions were making coffee runs and answering mail. I wasn't paid in money. I was paid in music. When new albums from record companies were sent to the station they often sent duplicates, and I got the extras. I had the most extensive album collection in the whole town.

One day the owner was there, and he was in an extremely agitated mood. The guy who did play-by-play for the little league playoff broadcast had quit without any notice, leaving the station in the lurch. Now the owner was going to have to announce the games himself, and he asked me if I'd like to come along and be his color man. I didn't have a lick of experience, but I was excited at the prospect of being on the air. I jumped at the chance. Besides, I figured if I screwed up, who the hell was listening to little league playoffs anyway?

When the game started, I quickly realized my broadcast partner didn't know shit about baseball. When a kid hit a sacrifice fly, the owner didn't know how to describe what transpired. I took over. After a while, I was doing the play-by-play and he was doing the color. Eventually, he let me carry the whole broadcast while he just read commercials.

On the ride home he thanked me for a job well done. He handed me forty dollars, then, out of the blue, made an announcement.

"I'm going to shut down the radio station, and sell the rights to the transmitter so someone else can use it," he said. "I'm tired of radio."

Of all the luck! My broadcasting career started and ended on the same day!

The next couple of months were bad. The lucky DJs got other radio jobs. The not-as-lucky took civilian gigs. TC's stable of women vanished overnight. It seemed even the strippers and wayward housewives wanted a guy with some kind of future. After the last broadcast, we stole as much stuff as we could carry. They locked the door behind us, and that was it.

The next week the station was a State Farm Insurance office.

\* \* \* \* \*

In college, I took basic classes. I quickly got used to the freedom of being away. I was most comfortable partying and doing late night barhopping. I declared psychology as my major. That was laughable because most of it went right over my head. Looking back now, had I followed through with that major, I'm sure I would have been my own best patient.

Communications seemed the easy choice for a rebound major, so I gravitated to something familiar, the school radio station. I took some writing classes and studied to get my first class FCC license. Doing afternoon drive radio was very comfortable for me. I never ran out of things to say, and I always played good music. Even though having a small following was kind of exciting, I kept remembering the jocks in my hometown like TC and how they didn't make shit. One in ten million seemed to get any notoriety, and the idea of hopping from town to town, station to station really didn't settle too well with me. But radio made me happy, and it gave me one hell of a record collection.

I graduated in May of 1981 with really only one option; to set the world of radio on its ear. I was going to be the next Howard Stern, before there was a Howard Stern. The cassette tape of my finest moments as a FM drive time DJ from the school station was sure to do that.

My tape consisted of brilliantly crafted intros and outs, commercial spots that were read with energy and exuberance, and that famous witty banter that once cultivated quite a following amongst my fellow students. Radio seemed a natural fit. All I had to do was just be me, charming with the right amount of bullshit.

The first opening I applied for was in Lake Geneva, Wisconsin, a small resort town between Chicago and Milwaukee. Lake Geneva was a place where wealthy Chicagoans had summer homes, perfect for a guy who didn't have two nickels to rub together. The trade magazine ad was for a DJ, afternoon drive, Monday through Friday. I had an unjustified confidence in my heart of hearts that the phone would ring, and off I'd go. I wasn't surprised at all when the station manager called.

I pulled into town on a warm summer morning. I scanned the radio dial, found my future station, and I cranked it. "Sweet Emotion" by Aerosmith blasted from the speakers of my 1974 Chevy Impala. It wasn't long before I came upon a huge antenna that loomed over a little brick building.

The building looked nothing like a radio station. It was more like a house with a big picture window. Inside the window, I thought I spied what looked like a twelve-year-old boy wearing headphones and operating the controls. I wondered if maybe there were two stations in town and that I should look for the other one.

When I got out of my car, he waved to me like we were old friends. I took a deep breath, straightened my five-year-old tan suit coat with matching tan pants and brown clip on tie (which totally looked like a real tie), and walked in. The first thing that hit me was that there was no receptionist to greet me in the lobby. There was no lobby. There was only a desk with a bell on it and two speakers mounted on a wall blaring the tail end of the Aerosmith song.

I rang the bell and out came the little fellow I saw in the studio's window. He greeted me with a huge smile and a handshake.

"Hello, I'm Randy. You must be Chuck?"

"I am," I said.

The little guy then took me into the studio. He was doing a shift and interviewing me at the same time. He motioned for me to be quiet, came out of the song, and cross-faded into a commercial.

"Sorry I have to interview you this way, but I'm station manager-slash morning DJ," he said. While he was writing things in his log and switching around carts for commercials, he looked up with a big smile on his face. "I'll cut to the chase. My first impression is that I like you and I enjoyed your tape. I would like to offer you the afternoon drive slot."

Normally, you would think someone out of school on his first interview would leap at any opportunity for employment. But I've always been a big fan of going with your gut, and my gut was screaming "no fucking way"! I smiled at the little fellow.

"Wow, that's great," I replied. How much?"

"Excuse me?"

"Yes, you know, money. How much?" I said, with a smile. Without looking at me, he cued up a record.

"The great thing about this station is that we get wild and break format every now and then and spin whatever we want to hear," he said, damn near yelling.

Lake Geneva was now getting served a heavy dose of Deep Purple. He played the record and took off his headset.

"Four hundred," he said.

I just stared at him.

"Four hundred a week?" I asked.

"No," he replied, "Four hundred a month."

There was nothing I could do but laugh.

"You're shitting me, right?" I asked.

He had a very solemn look on his face.

"I know it's low, but everyone who works here has two jobs. I bartend at night at a place called Jimmy's. It's a local pub, and I make just as much there as I do here. All told I work about seventy hours a week," he explained. The whole time he was looking at his shoes.

I had nothing to lose.

"I'm supposed to live on four hundred a month in a resort town? That's crazy," I said, raising my voice. I turned and started to walk out of the studio and into the next room before I realized it wasn't this guy's fault. He was just living his dream of being a DJ; just someone trying to make ends meet.

I reopened the studio door.

"Sorry man, I didn't mean to be a jerk, but you can probably make more shoveling shit in forty hours than you make in seventy hours the way you're doing it."

He cracked a smile at me.

"I know, but this is what I want to do with my life, and I'm going to give it an honest shot, you know?"

I nodded and smiled.

"I get it," I said, "I get it."

"Hey, Chuck," he said as I walking out, "Can you show the

next guy in please?"

Sure as shit, there was another guy waiting, and I'm sure another one after that. Someone was going to take that job, but it wasn't going to be me. I didn't know where I was going from there, but for the moment all I could think about was having a beer and putting this all behind me. So I hopped in the Chevy, ripped off the clip-on tie, unbuttoned the jacket, and rolled down the windows. That was when I realized I was in a resort town and couldn't even afford a beer.

I put the car in drive and drove home.

\* \* \* \* \*

You would think that experience would have been enough, but I was just dense enough to be persistent. My next stop on the DJ job hunt was another rock and roll station. This one was in a small town in central Illinois. I talked to the owner on the phone and set up a meeting. This guy uttered the word "Dude" at least thirty times during our phone conversation.

I walked up to the third floor radio station, located above a Chinese restaurant and a physical therapy clinic that looked like it specialized in happy endings. Again, my gut was telling me this would be a bad scene. The building was shit, there was peeling paint everywhere, and once again there wasn't even a reception area.

I smelled a combination of incense and pot as I opened the door and squinted through a haze of smoke. The studio was to the right, and the office was to the left. In the studio, a longhaired older guy was bobbing his head up and down to the melodic sounds of Jimi Hendrix. The guy in the office had a big bushy beard and long hair and was sucking the shit out of a bong.

I stood there for a moment before I also noticed a very pregnant woman in the corner of his office. She was smoking a cigarette, drinking a glass of wine, and looking totally out of it. Both of them were also getting into the music by Hendrix, swaying and singing along. After they noticed me, I was invited into the office.

"I'm Frank," the bong-sucker said, "and this is my old lady, Cheri." This guy was so messed up he could barely speak, and it was early in the afternoon. "I'm the President and CEO of FM 98.7, Central Illinois' powerhouse rock and roll radio station." He took another bong hit, stretched his arms outward, and smiled. "This is my kingdom."

He told me how much he liked my resume tape. I just kept looking at his wife, a haggard mess who was killing her unborn child with booze and cigarettes. In the midst of spewing random nonsense, Frank stood up.

"Get in the studio and show me your stuff!" he screamed.

"Excuse me?" I replied, stunned.

"You fucking heard me man," he said, waving his arms. "If you want to get into this game, then get in the studio and show me what you can do!"

I peered into the studio, and that gut feeling struck again.

"I'm not ready for that, and I'm not bumping the guy you have in there," I shot back.

Frank maneuvered himself from around his desk and got right in my face, pot breath and all.

"Fuck that!" The extremely stoned CEO yelled. "He doesn't

care. He does what he's told. Now get in there and show me your stuff!"

"First let me take a leak," I calmly said.

He smiled and sat back down. As I was walking away I noticed his "Old Lady" face down on the desk, drink in hand, ready to give birth at any moment.

This was a bad place to be.

I hit the front door and never looked back.

# Chapter

# SUDDENLY A CAMERAMAN

With no prospects of anything and the reality sinking in that I may be a permanent fixture at Mom and Dad's house, I was excited when a friend of my mother's called one day. She said she knew the news director of a television station in Rockford, Illinois and they had an opening for a cameraman. Now there was something I knew nothing about.

The thought of being unemployed and living in my parents' basement all my adult life might have been appealing, but it obviously wasn't in my long-term plans. It was time to man up, get serious, and give this my full attention. I could be a cameraman, right? It had to beat hard labor. I decided to go for it. My mother's friend hooked me up with a woman named Laurie for a phone interview.

Laurie was news director for the station and had one of the sexiest phone voices I ever heard. This woman could have made a fortune in the phone sex business. I talked to her for about forty minutes.

"Listen, you sound like a good guy," she said. "I'm looking for someone normal, someone we can train, not someone with an attitude. Camera guys have egos. I don't need that shit. We need someone we can mold our way, our style. Are you my guy?"

"I'm your guy," I said.

"Outstanding!" she replied. "See you in two days. You need to meet with my chief photographer. If you're good with him, the job is yours."

The DJ thing fell by the wayside the second I sat in the lobby of the television station. The appeal of chasing news stories around the city seemed exciting.

As I waited, I noticed the pictures of the air talent on the lobby wall. There was a picture of a really fat guy with a huge nose wearing an ill-fitting corduroy suit. There was a guy with a Hitler mustache and tall hair. And there was also Hispanic guy who looked like Ricky Ricardo. He had slicked-back pitch black hair and was wearing one of those real wide collared disco shirts. As I sat looked at the all the pictures of the employees and the NBC Logo on the wall, I realized something.

This was a real job. It my first interview with a lobby, my first interview with a receptionist, a smoking hot one no less. This was it. If I fucked this up, my next interview was going to be at the post office or the grocery store.

Suddenly, I heard a voice coming around a corner and there he was: the spitting image of Ricky Ricardo.

"Hello, Chuck. I'm Terence Lopez, managing editor, and news reporter. Follow me. I'll show you around." We walked around the station, and he explained a few things. "The job doesn't pay much—only $4.50 an hour–but in a couple years, with the experience you get here, you'll be ready to move to a bigger market and make a lot more money."

"How long have you been here?" I asked.

"Eleven years," he replied. I guess he didn't subscribe to his own theory.

Terence then took me to a back room where he introduced me to the Chief Photographer, Bill. Bill picked up a film camera, set it on a workbench, and gave me the once-over.

"Laurie said you're all right," he said after a short uncomfortable silence, "and that's good enough for me. You start Monday. I'll teach you how to shoot and how to be a news cameraman."

"That's it?" I asked. "You're hiring me?"

"Yup. Listen, for $4.50 an hour it's no big risk on our part. Know what I mean?"

Bill shook my hand and walked away.

I had a job.

\* \* \* \* \*

I learned a lot from Bill. He was a stand-up guy and a great photographer. At the time, we were one of the last stations in the country that was still using film cameras. The thing about film was that you had to load the magazines with reels of three hundred feet of film every day in a dark room. A person with skill and a sense of touch could maneuver around the pitch-black area with no problem and load magazine after magazine in a short period of time.

I was not that person.

For me, it was a struggle every day. I had to take the film from a sealed bag, open the metal case, put the film in, and loop it through the magazine, then close it and make sure it was sealed properly to make sure there wouldn't be any light leaks. And I had to do it in the darkness.

Thank God for Bill. It was his daily ritual to knock on the

door to tell me to calm down; things would be all right. Every day, I would drop the film all over the floor in the dark. Then I would have to manually wind it back up and somehow fit it in the magazine. I sucked at it and would curse a blue streak until his compassionate voice would calm me down.

"It's a hundred dollars a roll, numb nut," Bill would yell. "Make it right, or I'll have your ass."

As time went by, loading the film became second nature. I was getting into the job. I learned the standard shots, how to react in certain situations, and what it took to make a complete news story. Editing film turned out to be a fun process. The reporter would tell you they needed thirty seconds of footage and a sound bite. He or she would then cut a voice track on an audio cart that was exactly 30 seconds long. That voice track would be played over the edited footage. The timing had to be perfect. The audio man had to be right on the money, or it would turn in to a bad Japanese movie.

The editing, cutting, and gluing the filmstrips together along with timing everything out was very labor intensive. I made a habit out of watching our four o'clock news every day in the break room when my job was complete. Granted, I was new to this game, but even a rookie can tell when something looks like shit, and three out of five times, it looked like shit. The audio track was always out-of-sync with the footage. Every time it happened I would look around the room to see if there was a reaction from anyone. I was amazed no one ever said a thing.

This went on for quite a while, and it was really starting to bother me, so I went to the only person I knew with any kind of common sense at all: my man Bill. After I expressed my concerns to him he laughed and suggested that I go into the control room the next day, introduce myself to the audio man and watch him do his job.

"You do that," Bill said, "and you'll have a better understanding of how this place operates."

So I did. The next day I got my work done, waltzed right into the control room and patiently stood next to the audio board. Within minutes a large looming figure appeared through the door of the darkened area carrying a cup of coffee and a newspaper. As he got closer, I got a better look at him. He was a Native American with a ponytail wearing a big turquoise necklace and matching rings. I couldn't help but stare. In the dimly lit room I struggled to make out his face. He stuck his hand out and said his name was Joel. I told him I was new on the job and was checking things out.

"I've never really seen a control room, let alone an audio board," I offered. "Could I observe you working the board?"

He made a grunting noise. That, I assumed, meant yes. I had been watching for a couple of minutes when Joel leaned over and turned on a small light above the audio board. The brightness of the light gave me a better look at my new friend. Besides the jewelry, he was wearing a sharp looking long-sleeved suede shirt with some cool designs on it. He was also wearing something else.

The audio man wore hearing aids in both ears.

How in God's name can you have a hard-of-hearing audio man?

The show's open began. The intro music was too loud. The anchor's microphone was low. The sound was off for the first story. I looked around the control room, and not a soul said a word. Nothing. All I could hear was the director calling camera shots.

I looked at Joel, and he was cool as a cucumber. I just wanted to yell to everyone in the room "What the fuck is wrong with you people? The guy can't hear! Get a different audio man."

But I didn't. I just stepped back and left the room. I was gutless like all the rest. And to be honest, he may have been a bit older, but I wasn't going to screw with someone that looked that tough. I made my way back to the camera room and sat down. Bill walked in a few moments later.

"Well, what did you learn in there?" he asked.

"I've never seen such a thing," I said.

"Joel's a great guy who's close to retirement," Bill explained, smiling. "There are only three stations in town, and we all make money no matter what goes on the air. Good news, shit news, it doesn't matter. Pay your dues, get the experience you need, and get a job in a bigger market where you can make some real dough and have somewhat of a future. That's my advice."

With that, he turned and walked away. Smart man, I thought. I realized that I needed to get into a top five market to make some good money, but if I somehow screwed that up, I could always stay here and be another knucklehead getting a paycheck.

*   *   *   *   *

As time passed, I got pretty good at this photography thing. Film went away and was replaced by videotape. With video, you could be a lot more creative with shooting and editing. As my confidence grew, I would get more daring and aggressive. I actually began to get a grasp on this thing.

I covered two separate fires in the middle of winter. At the first fire, I wanted to give the viewer at home the unique perspective of what a fire looks like from inside a burning house.

Here's how that happened. I was on call, an honor each cameraman got twice a year for a month at a time. The cameraman on call got a company car, all the camera equipment, and a pager. When the pager went off, it was go time. You'd get an address to the latest car crash, fire, or shooting. That first night, I had just made a new blonde friend in a local pub, and we were both extremely over served.

When the pager went off, I had no clue where this address was. Luckily, my newfound buddy was a lifelong resident and guided me to the proper address. When we got there, I noticed the upper half of the two-story house was on fire. Eager to impress my co-pilot, I instructed her to stay near the car for her own safety. I grabbed the camera and ran toward the soon to be raging inferno. As I got close to the front of the house, a group of firemen had just punched open the front door. I was caught up in the moment (not to mention somewhat loaded), so I decided following the firemen into the burning building was a good idea. As soon as I stepped inside, everything turned pitch black. The room was filled with smoke. The fire was still contained to the upper half of the house. The fireman's flashlights weren't giving them enough light to see through the dark and the smoke. They didn't notice me behind them until I turned on my camera light. The second I hit that baby the whole first floor became filled with light.

"Thanks buddy, just what we needed," one of the fireman said.

"Holy shit," I thought. "I hit the mother lode."

I was blending in with the firemen. I was videotaping the inside of a house while it was actually on fire. But as time wore on, the booze started wearing off, and I realized how stupid I was being. The firemen had fought their way up the stairs to tackle the fire still confined to the upper half of the house. I started to back away, slowly moving toward the front door. All of a sudden, I heard a giant creak, and a huge crash. A beam from the ceiling fell and landed about three feet from where I was standing. I looked up and saw the whole ceiling was starting to catch on fire. Like a true pro I panned my camera upward to show the spreading flames as they engulfed the structure above me. Suddenly I felt a sharp pain in the back of my neck.

"You fucking asshole! What in the fuck are you doing here?" The fire captain yelled at me. "Get out before I have you arrested!"

He grabbed me by the neck and spun me right out the front door. Without missing a beat, I hopped off the porch and started shooting exteriors of the house as it started burning out of control.

This story does have a happy ending, I suppose. All of the firemen got out safely. The family who owned the home was away for the weekend, so no one died or was injured. The house was a total loss, but it wasn't really a news story. On the other hand, I had some awesome footage, and my new blonde friend thought I was damn brave for going into the burning home. Stupidity has its rewards.

* * * * *

Just a few weeks later, I made dumb move number two. It

was early afternoon on a very cold February day. The wind chill was below zero, super cold and very dangerous. As luck would have it, I was sent to another house fire in a brand new subdivision. Evidently some faulty wiring caused this one, and the structure was really burning.

This time I was sober. I had vowed to never stupidly run into a burning building again, so I stayed across the street shooting the whole thing on a tripod. It was the perfect vantage point. I had great shots of the firemen going in and out of the house. The fire trucks had hoses strewn across the front yard. Water was spraying from the couplings and instantly freezing when it hit the ground.

After being there for only fifteen minutes, I began losing feeling in everything but my left ear lobe. My body said to me, "you have time for one more shot." I wanted it to be an artsy picture to open the news story, a picture to stun the viewer's visual senses.

I scanned the scene and found what I needed. At the top of the roof, a firefighter was using his axe to make a ventilation hole. It was perfect. The man was backlit by the sun with just the right amount of smoke and haze surrounding him. After focusing on the man and framing it just perfectly, I rolled the camera. This was the shot of the year.

I would have wept for joy, but my tear ducts were frozen solid. I must have rolled tape on that guy for almost three minutes and was going to give it about five-seconds more, when out of nowhere I heard a loud popping sound. Flames burst right through the roof. In an instant, the fireman was gone. Everyone started screaming. It was chaos.

Taking the camera off the tripod in record time, I ran across the street and headed toward the backyard. I jumped over the scattered hoses, slid across the frozen ground, and followed two firemen through the backyard gate. A handful of firefighters were standing around one lone firefighter. The fireman who had been on the roof moments ago was now in a snow bank, and he was smiling.

From my vantage point it had looked as if he went through the roof, but apparently when the fire shot through the roof, he had only lost his balance and slid downward across the frozen shingles. He had caught the gutter on his way down and dropped safely to the ground from the second story.

That was one lucky bastard.

As the firefighters stood around and watched the second story burn, I decided to move further back in the yard to take a wide shot with the firemen and the burning roof in the frame. Looking through the viewfinder with my right eye, my left eye noticed a giant cloud of smoke starting to engulf the entire backyard. A strong icy wind had picked up and drove the smoke from the burning roof right at us.

"Quick, put on your masks!" a fireman yelled.

In an instant, the firemen all dropped to a knee and put on their oxygen masks. Now imagine the feeling I had when I saw a giant cloud coming at me. There wasn't a damn thing I could do about it. I had absolutely nowhere to go, and this thing, this cloud of smoke, was over me in a heartbeat. I could see nothing. I held my breath and started walking in the white haze. Realizing I had the lung capacity of a sparrow, I figured maybe I could hold out maybe forty-seconds before I would be launched into a choking, convulsing fit.

Disoriented and really starting to panic, I considered dropping the camera to lighten my load, but I was too big of a pussy to leave the camera behind. If something happened to it, I would have been fired from my $4.50 an hour job. So, with the camera in tow I headed toward where I thought the firemen were. Unfortunately, I was too twisted around to even know what direction I was going.

"How in the hell could I be overcome by smoke in the outdoors?" I thought to myself.

I envisioned being found next to the swing set in the fetal position with frozen tears on my face. This was a bullshit way to die. People would laugh at my funeral. On my tombstone it would just say, "Stupid."

Suddenly someone grabbed me and put a mask over my face. It was a fireman! By the grace of God, he had somehow bumped into me. The two of us just stood there for what seemed like forever trading the mask back and forth. Slowly the smoke started to dissipate.

When things cleared, he looked at me with a sad expression on his face.

"I'm screwed," he said. "These guys are going to fuck with me something fierce."

"Why would they do that? You saved my ass."

"I'm a pro-bee, the new guy," he said with a trembling voice. "I just started the job and made a dumb mistake. In the cold air the smoke will choke you, even outdoors. You're supposed to put on the mask and stay low."

"Seriously?" I asked. "They will screw with you just because you got lost in some smoke?"

"Look at them," he said as he pointed to a group of firemen standing next to what was left of the house. They were laughing and pointing at my newfound savior. The chief emerged from the middle of the pack holding a fire helmet.

"Shit, that's mine," said my new hero.

As he started to walk away, he turned toward me.

"No offense," he said, "but I wish I never bumped into you."

He walked toward the other firemen, catching all kinds of shit the entire way.

Needless to say, that wasn't exactly a heartwarming moment for me. Here was a guy who had just saved my life.

And he totally regretted it.

Chapter

 **TIME TO LEAVE**

Recording all the network news shows every night and watching how those guys shot their stories had really helped me. Other people started to notice my work. Every day I felt more confident, and the compliments from my bosses became more frequent.

One night, I received a call from a news director in Columbus, Ohio. He had been passing through town and saw a story I shot, a day in the life of local paramedics. The news director called my station to track me down because he had a job opening and wanted to talk to me about it. After agreeing to meet him for drinks, my mind wandered. I was pulling down a mind-boggling twelve grand. What if I doubled that?

I would still be dirt poor, but this would be a giant leap forward financially. I didn't tell a soul about my secret negotiations. I met him at a local pub, nothing fancy, just a shot and beer joint. I spotted him immediately: God-awful toupee, big Elton John type glasses, a bad sweater vest, and a giant pinky ring.

He told me he'd worked in several television markets, although I noticed he never quite said which markets. He had an arrogant tone in his deep voice, but this guy had small market written all over him. He boasted he'd done it all, from janitor to cameraman, from reporter to main anchor. And now he was a news director.

"You are looking at the face of television news," he said.

The more he talked, the more I drank. He kept leaning over the table and violating my personal space. At one point he said the following, hand to God.

"Think of me as George Steinbrenner, and I'm here to sign you to play for the New York Yankees of television news."

Now I hadn't seen much of the world, but Columbus, Ohio sure didn't sound like the big leagues. Steinbrenner wouldn't have pissed on a guy like this if he was on fire. After about thirty minutes, this windbag told me I would become a better cameraman if I moved to Columbus. Under his tutelage, he promised I would become one of the all-time greats.

God's gift to television news then slid my fourth beer across the table, accompanied by an offer of sixteen grand. I remember looking at him and not saying a word. The jukebox was playing, and glasses were clinking. People were talking and laughing. I had just given him close to an hour of my life that I would never get back. I just sat there and didn't say a word.

"Money not enough?" he asked.

I looked him right in the eye. "It's only a couple grand more than I make now," I replied, "and I don't think that's worth a move."

He stared at me then motioned to the waitress for the check. "Sorry, but that's my best offer. Great to meet you. Good luck in your career."

He paid the waitress and left.

\* \* \* \* \*

Now, in the past I would have been upset and a little panicky from this experience, but this time, it really didn't bother me in the slightest. I looked at this experience as a motivator. I didn't want to be like this guy from Columbus. I decided right there and then that since I grew up watching Chicago television, that's where I was going to go. From that moment forward, everything I did was going to be with a resume tape in mind. I was really going to bear down, do first class work, and get to the top of the game.

Unfortunately I also liked to screw around and laugh, and that was somewhat of a deterrent for my new found dedication. One of the reasons I couldn't keep focused on my exit plan was a reporter named Rob Sherman. Imagine if you will, a three hundred pound man with food crumbs stuck to the side of his mouth, squeezed into plaid sweater vests and suit coats that were way too small.

Rob was a staple in Rockford television and radio before that. He was a veteran reporter who wrote with great flair and passion, but he could also be the silliest bastard you ever met. On the other hand, Rob was also a tragic figure. When he was a young radio reporter, he had the unspeakable misfortune of covering his first wife and child's death in a horrible car accident. They say that he was never the same. There were times I'd watch him from a distance, and I could see the sadness in his eyes.

One day in the newsroom we heard over the scanners that the sheriff's department was sending an officer to the outskirts of town. The scanner traffic reported a body in a field. In a flash, Rob burst from his seat.

"It's you and me, crime fighter! Maybe it's a murder that will liven up our day. You can put that on your resume tape!"

Rob threw on his jacket and ran for the door. When we were in the car, and traveling at a high speed, Rob stuck his head out the passenger side window, and with the chilly winter air hitting him in the face, crazy Rob started making noises like a police siren. In congested traffic, the noises got louder and louder. Sometimes my overweight friend would just yell "motherfucker" out the window as we passed other cars.

I remember looking at him, wondering what the hell was wrong with him. He looked like a dog with his head hanging out the open window, just enjoying the moment. Once we pulled up to the scene, we noticed an empty police car at the edge of a cornfield. In the distance we spotted an officer about one hundred yards away in the middle of the field.

"That's a long walk in this cold. Have fun!" Rob said.

"All right, douche bag," I replied. "You stay here and keep your fat ass warm."

I hopped out of the car and grabbed the camera.

"Wait up," he yelled, as I knew he would.

"It's been a while since I've seen a stiffy." Rob looked at me and smiled. "Don't say a fucking word. I know what you're thinking."

We made our way through the snowy frozen field, crunching through the snow, fighting the howling frozen wind. It felt like we were moving but never quite going anywhere. When we got closer to the kneeling officer we could see the victim, an elderly man bent over with his pants around his ankles.

"Jesus Christ, look at that, that's a terrible way to go," Rob said.

The officer overheard my large friend and nodded his head.

"Looks to me he died trying to take a dump," he said.

"That's how Elvis went!" Rob chimed in.

I knelt down to get a closer look. The poor guy was frozen solid; his face and hands were white and stiff.

"How did he get out here," I asked?

The officer had one of those cool trooper hats with the earflaps like they wore in the movie Fargo.

"My best guess is he wandered away from the Lutheran Nursing Home about a mile away from here last night," he said. "The poor fuck dropped his pajamas to take a shit and that's all she wrote. Heart attack I'm sure, just like Elvis."

"How would you like to be the person at the nursing home responsible for him? Imagine making that call to his family," Rob said.

The three of us stood there for the longest time just looking at this poor bastard. I didn't know what say. The Christian thing to do was say a prayer. We needed to say something to mark his time on earth. Suddenly, I heard a sniffle. I glanced at Rob who was wiping his nose and rubbing his eyes. The big man appeared to be caught up in the moment.

I waited for a few words of wisdom to come from the long time journalist. This was a man who was familiar with death and hardship, a man who could expound on the moment and share some personal experience. Rob inhaled and exhaled. You could see his breath in the cold. Slowly he cleared his throat. Rob then proceeded to bark out the most compassionate and eloquent tribute ever given in the history of tributes.

"Fuck this, let's get some lunch."

\* \* \* \* \*

The more experience I got, the more comfortable I became. One day towards the end of 1983, I covered a story about food stamps and discovered I was actually qualified to receive them. I was the working poor.

I sent out resume tapes continually, with no luck. My first tip on job networking came from a guy who did repair work on the station's transmitter. He had a buddy named Andy who had been working in the maintenance department at NBC in Chicago for the past couple of years. Andy gave me some solid info on how to get my foot in the door. He pointed out that 1984 was going to be a big year work-wise for NBC. It was a Presidential election year, and the station was going to be hiring quite a few people. He gave me the names and internal phone numbers of all the big hitters, most importantly a man named Rick Harvey. A former network cameraman himself, Rick was the boss of all the news technicians on the street for NBC.

I sent him a tape of my work and started calling incessantly, but Rick had one barracuda of a secretary. She was smart and stubborn and would never put my calls through. She knew I was just calling to bother him for a job, so she blocked my every attempt.

"Rick is in a meeting," was her catch phrase. That woman was good at her job and it made me nuts. One day I got lucky and caught him when the barracuda was out. Rick told me he had received my tape and that he would look at it in February of 1984.

"I'll be hiring people in April," he said.

We shot the breeze for about ten minutes. Rick told me

about the hiring procedures, then right before we hung up he said the words I longed to hear.

"Get back to me mid-January; we'll talk some more."

I can't remember exactly how I responded, but I think it was "Thank you. Thank you. Thank you. Thank you. Thank you. Thank you." I also might have also said, "Thank you."

Now I was just biding my time in Rockford.

\* \* \* \* \*

After our station in Rockford posted a slight drop in the ratings, Terence Lopez, managing editor and reporter and Ricky Ricardo look-a-like decided to impose his will on the viewers of northern Illinois. The self-appointed "best reporter in town" announced he was coming out of mothballs with the hopes of skyrocketing our station to number one status in the market.

As luck would have it I was the guy who got to work with Cronkite Jr. Every day, he covered one lame story after the next. It seemed the best reporter in town wouldn't know a good news story if it bit him in the ass of his designer jeans.

I have two favorite Terence stories.

One time, we were doing a live shot in a high school when a kid at the opposite end of the empty hallway dropped his books making a loud banging noise. This froze the future Tom Brokaw dead in his tracks. He was so stunned he couldn't speak, and his eyes got as big as saucers. He stammered and stuttered. This was live television at its finest, total silence with an occasional gasp for air. Not a word was spoken from the anchor team back at the station. The director was silent. Terence was blank. He had nothing.

The guy in the truck started whispering to me in my headset. He went from being respectfully quiet to laughing hysterically in my ear. Both of us couldn't believe how far this had gone. It had to be closing in on 45 seconds before the anchor finally stepped in, with a shit-eating grin on his face.

"We are having technical problems," he said. "We'll get back to Terence later."

"You're clear," the director said into Terrence's ear while laughing.

I shut off the camera and looked at the city's best reporter. Terence set down the microphone walked out of the school. He caught a cab and went home. Later that night I went back to the station to find out that everyone involved in that show took great delight in his fuck up. When he froze on the air the whole station went nuts. The director just let him hang. Television really can be a cold business. To this day, they still have that live shot on a gag reel that's played at the company Christmas party.

The next little adventure happened on a chilly Friday night. I was paired with Terence and our sports anchor Rick Whitman. Terence was doing a feature story on a big high school cross-town rivalry football game. Rick tagged along to get an interview with one of the coaches.

Our television station was located on the outskirts of town, farmland on unpaved roads. As we headed back to the station, we came upon a really bad accident. A car missed turning on a curve and went straight into a telephone pole.

I stopped the car, grabbed my camera, and got right up to the wreckage. The first cop on the scene asked me to shine my camera light inside the darkened car to see if there were any survivors. I cautiously stepped closer to the passenger side and pointed the camera where the window had busted out. There were two young high school girls wearing cheerleading outfits covered in blood.

Dead.

In the backseat I could see beer cans, and the whole car smelled of alcohol. It looked like the steering wheel went right into the driver's chest. (This was before airbags had been invented.) The second girl was sitting in the middle of the front seat, and it looked like she had hit her head on the windshield or the dash. As I panned the camera around, I noticed the glass was blown out on the passenger side. I really didn't think much of it at first. There was just so much blood.  More police showed up, and I backed off a little as Terence came over to join me.

Terence started peering into the car with his hand over his mouth. Rick, on the other hand, was about twenty feet back, not really caring one way or another.

I stepped back to get a wide shot of the car in the darkness. It felt like I was standing on a small pile of dirt or sand. Terence wanted to stay out of the shot, so he stood next to me. I pointed the camera down toward the ground using the light to see what I was standing on. It was an arm of another dead girl. That scared the shit out of me, but I kept it together. Terence, on the other hand, started screaming like a little girl at a surprise party. I had never heard a man scream like that. The cops came running over to see what had made him scream.

Terence stood motionless with his mouth open. He was hyperventilating. His reaction caught us all by surprise. Rick burst out laughing, which considering the situation, was admittedly somewhat inappropriate. Terence staggered toward Rick and grabbed him. Suddenly, with a moan and a belch, Terence vomited all over himself and Rick. The mild-mannered sportscaster instinctively pushed Terence away and in the process, grabbed Terence by the collar of his shirt and twisted it, inadvertently choking him. Terence briefly struggled then broke free from Rick's grasp.

As Terrence staggered around in a circle, Rick started yelling and cursing a blue streak. He lunged toward the rubber legged reporter to pummel him but was intercepted by the police at the last second.

The cops got right in Rick's face, forcing him to retreat to our car. Terence was teary-eyed; his pants and boots were covered in puke. He was quivering.

"Please get me out of here," he sobbed.

We cautiously headed back to the car, not really knowing what Rick was going to do next. I carefully opened the driver side door. Rick was sitting in the middle of the back seat. I could vaguely make out his features by the car's dome light.

"Rick, are we all right?" I asked.

"We're fine," he replied from his dark surroundings. "Let's leave."

Terence very cautiously slid into the front passenger seat and off we went. We drove in deafening silence through the night. Every now and then, a car would pass and illuminate Rick's graying hair in the rearview mirror. Finally, he spoke. Rick started muttering that he saw bodies like that in Vietnam. Death was a way of life.

"I was a machine gunner," he said, "and in combat the life expectancy of the guy with the big machine gun was about two minutes in a firefight. No sooner would I give the next guy the gun, and he would die. I'd get it right back."

I imagined Rick driving a bayonet into my neck, before pulling the car to the side of the road and making Terence eat his own testicles. As we pulled into the station, I got brave. I made eye contact with Rick in the rear view mirror.

"By chance are you on any medication?" I asked.

"Prozac and Zoloft calm me down," he said with a steely glare, "but the assholes in the sports department keep stealing it."

The car stopped, Rick hopped out and tapped on the passenger side window where Terence was still trembling in fear. Terence cautiously lowered the window.

"Sorry," Rick said. "I lost my head, the blood and all. I didn't mean to go off on you. You're a good fella. Just toughen up."

He gave us a deranged smile and walked away. Terence turned to me with puffy eyes and cracked a slight smile.

"Man, you stepped on a dead girl," he whispered. "I never saw that before".

He was right, and the sad thing was that with all the crazy shit I went through with those two idiots, I hadn't given it a second thought. I had become hardened to the things I was seeing on the streets. Dead people had become part of the job. It was something that didn't bother me anymore, and that really bothered me.

\* \* \* \* \*

Winter had fully set in, and the year was coming to a close. The guy in Chicago told me get back to him in January, but I was an impatient bastard and needed a little reinforcement. I decided to go for broke. On December 23, 1983 before I left work to attend my company Christmas party, I dialed Rick Harvey's office. This time the call was not intended for Rick; I wanted to make peace with the barracuda. She picked up after two rings.

"Merry Christmas, Rick Harvey's office. This is Nicole."

"Nicole, this is Chuck from the Rockford station," I responded. "Please don't hang up; I want to talk to you."

"Rick isn't in," she said. "He's off for two weeks. I can't help you."

"I figured," I said. "I just wanted you to know that I didn't mean to be a bother. I know you've gotten a ton of phone calls from me, and I realize you're just doing your job, but I hope you understand this is something I will not give up on. I know it sounds like a cliché, but this what I truly want. Did you ever want something that bad?"

There was silence on the other end of the line, followed by what sounded like a sigh.

"Hang on a minute," she said. "I'll be right back."

She put me on hold. Now I was thinking I really had screwed up. I had pissed off the barracuda. But it was too late to turn back. A good two minutes passed before she came back.

"Rockford, right?" she asked.

"Rockford, yes," I answered.

"You're in the good pile," she said. "You'll be getting a call."

"How can that be?" I asked, "Rick said the tapes don't get looked at until February."

"I'm telling you they were already looked at. He likes your work. Merry Christmas."

Stunned, my heart started racing.

"Thank you," was the best reply I could give.

"My goal is to be an actor," she said quietly. "I've had tons of disappointment. I get it. I hope this makes your holiday. Call after the New Year, and you owe me."

\* \* \* \* \*

I remember having that drunken feeling at the Christmas party before I even touched a drop. I was ecstatic as I walked around the restaurant saying hello to everyone. I stood in the corner and carefully surveyed the room. We were in a small Italian joint, one of those great little neighborhood places. Christmas lights and holiday decorations covered every inch of that restaurant. It was a very festive atmosphere. People were laughing and joking and really drinking hard. Terence went from table to table, smiling and wishing everyone "Happy Holidays."

I also noticed the kindly old man who said hello to me every workday. That evening I noticed something very different about him: he was with a woman at least twenty-five years younger than him, and he looked happy as hell. The man's name was Fred, and he had to be at least sixty-five years old. He was a small man with a flat top haircut and glasses, and he walked a little hunched over. Fred spoke very softly, and very precisely.

As I stared at the young woman with him, I thought back to other company functions and realized he had never come with the same woman twice. He had a new babe each time, one younger than the next. I consulted my cameramen colleague Bill, who knew where all the bodies were buried.

"What's the deal with Fred and the younger women?" I asked. Bill chuckled. "You've never heard the legend of Fred?"

Apparently Fred dated one of the station's secretaries years ago, and she was also quite a bit younger. After a three-day weekend at some resort, she told a few friends that Fred was a gifted man. So much so, she had developed a few problems and had to seek medical attention after their little 'rendezvous.'

Her estimates put the old guy at around a foot long. Fred seems to have served all of northern Illinois, never wanting to settle down. I had looked at him like he was somebody's grand-father, not John Holmes, Jr.

\* \* \* \* \*

Before I knew it, it was January. I was forming a real disdain for the job and all that it entailed. We were doing nightly live shots in the freezing cold to tell everybody that it was cold out and warn them not to venture into the dangerous tundra. It must be quite amusing to be sitting in your warm living room, watching some stupid douchebag pointing to a bank thermom-eter with chattering teeth. I was the guy running the camera with the douchebag. Mentally, I was already gone from there, but there hadn't been a phone call from Chicago yet, and I was nervously biding my time.

One night, I turned on the television just in time to catch our news. As the show open faded, our main anchor Bruce Roberts, with his trademark helmet hairdo, semi-excessive makeup, and equally bad NBC maroon blazer, introduced the top story of the day. A loud shrill scream came from off cam-era. Apparently, the TelePrompter had short-circuited and electrocuted the operator. Bruce paused until the man stopped screaming, shook his head, muttered "Jesus Christ," then continued with the newscast. I watched in disbelief. Only on a small station would you see something like that.

Our place had its characters, but one that stuck out was a fellow cameraman, Kurt. He was fixated on Fred, the senior citizen stud. The two of them had become good buddies. It was an odd friendship. Kurt was twenty-two, and Fred was at least forty years older. But these two would have lunch together and get into long-winded conversations about life experiences. Kurt was convinced his older friend had the power of persuasion over women, and Kurt wanted whatever Fred had to rub off on him. Kurt tried to persuade us that all those women were with him because our man Fred just knew what women wanted and he was treating them with the respect they deserved. In Kurt's eyes it had nothing to do with the fact that Fred was hung like a palm tree in a windstorm.

While the Kurt/Fred relationship blossomed, I still called Chicago once a week and became good phone pals with Nicole. She kept me informed about the progress. I felt good about my chances. One day in late March I was paged on the overhead sound system at work. I had a call. That call changed my life.

"Chuck, this is Rick Harvey, we'd like you to come to Chicago and work for us. Need you here in a week, get you up and running," Rick said.

"A week? I don't know," I replied, "that's a little short notice for the job I have now."

"Here's the deal," Rick countered. "We are hiring ninety-five people for summer relief jobs: cameramen, writers, directors, you name it. When it's over we will have just a few full-time jobs to offer. We'll keep the best of the best. Get here in one week, you'll get nine months guaranteed work. Make us wait two weeks, and you'll only get a six-month guarantee."

It took me about one second to answer.

"I'll be there in a week."

One-week notice is a bit of a shitty thing to do if you've been at a job for almost three years, but I had no choice, and the people who mattered most to me understood. Rob seemed very sad I was going, very few jokes. It saddened me to think I might never see my funny friend again. Kurt got a job with a production house in Los Angeles right about the same time. He also gave a week's notice, and his attitude was "fuck the station." He didn't care.

I cared, and I didn't realize how much until it was time to leave. This group of people had become part of my life, and I was leaving them behind forever. On the last day after the five o'clock show, Bill brought in a case of beer, and we all just sat around bullshitting and laughing. At one point he made a toast, and with a shit-eating smile on his face, Bill mustered up all sentiment one human could possible dedicate to another. He demanded silence and the attention of all present.

"To Chuck," he simply said. "Good luck, buddy."

Everyone applauded. Terence gave me a wave goodbye. Rob gave me a bear hug and told me to write. The place I wanted to leave for so long seemed like a place I now wanted to stay. After thanking everyone, I grabbed my coat and headed toward the door. Going through the lobby Fred stopped me, shook my hand, and wished me good luck. Fred looked sad, because he was losing his good friend Kurt. Kurt didn't want any part of the farewell party. He said goodbye to the people he liked and to hell with the rest. Fred excused himself and headed for the restroom. Kurt was grabbing his coat, also about to leave. He wished me good luck.

"Hey, don't you want to find out?" I asked.

"Find out what?" Kurt inquired.

"He's in the can. See if it's true. It's your last chance," I said laughing.

"Looking at that old man's Johnson is gay," he replied.

"All this time you said the rumor was bullshit. It wasn't what he was packing; it was his personality," I reminded him.

Kurt put his head down and went in. I waited for a good two minutes. Fred came out first. Ten-seconds later, a pale and somewhat bewildered Kurt exited.

"Well?" I asked.

"It's true," Kurt admitted. "He's all dick. It's the biggest thing I've ever seen. That old man is huge. Guess it's not his gift of gab. I stood next to him at the urinal, and I looked." Kurt paused. "Does that make me queer?"

"Yes, it does," I answered.

With that, I headed for the door. In the parking lot, I ran into anchorman Bruce Roberts. He was still donning his tacky maroon blazer.

"I'm going to the strip joint down the road for dinner," he said. "Get you a lap dance as a going away present?"

"Thanks Bruce," I replied. "Have to take a pass. Take care, buddy."

That sealed it for me. It was time to get out of town.

Who has dinner at a strip joint?

# Chapter

# HELLO CHI-TOWN

In April of 1984, I, along with four other new guys, reported to the mini-cam, an area that housed all the news cameramen. It was a totally different atmosphere than Rockford. This was the big time. NBC Chicago was where grown men worked in real careers. From the beginning it seemed the older guys in the shop viewed us younger guys as somewhat of a threat to their existence. I never wanted to be a threat to anyone. I just wanted to make some real money, and the real money was here. This was a union shop. Most of the guys made a lot of overtime. There was the potential to make a good living in this city. I had never wanted something as badly as I wanted this.

We worked as two-man crews. The sound guy handled the recorder and was responsible for the microphones and getting the best possible sound. The cameraman was expected to always be on top of his game and not miss a thing. His number one job was to get "the shot" every single time.

My first partner was a very skilled audio man named Gerald. Management thought it would be best for the older guys to work with the younger guys, to explain the system and show us the company way of thinking.

Gerald was a 50-something-year-old African-American, had a black belt in karate, never cursed, and when he spoke, his eyes would widen as he emphasized his point. Gerald's personal car was old Chevy Nova with over a hundred thousand miles on it and proudly never changed the oil. Gerald at one point had been a network soundman and had pretty much seen the world. He had a lifetime of television experience.

He was a bit angry at first to be working with a rookie, but we cut through the awkwardness rather quickly and became fast friends. Once I proved myself to him, Gerald spread the word amongst the older guys that I was all right, and they slowly started speaking to me as we covered general news, press conferences, and city council meetings.

At the time, Harold Washington had recently become the city's first black mayor, and the majority of the city council was white. Covering the council meetings was like watching a chess match, and the old vets showed me how things were done. Every issue started out as a simple debate. The debate led to accusations. The accusations led to backroom meetings, and the meetings eventually led to a deal.

Race was the big factor back then and still is in Chicago. I got a my first taste of the hardness of the big city one day when a man was holding his family hostage in a housing project, near the south Loop. Gerald took the call over the radio, threw on his seat belt, and hit the gas. When it came to breaking news, the speed limit was not a factor to him. We flew through the side streets of the neighborhoods. As we got closer, Gerald swung his right arm toward the back seat, making repeated attempts to grab something.

"Man, help me, will you?" he pleaded. "Grab the vests in the bag."

There was duffel bag with bulletproof vests on the back seat.

"Shit, Gerald," I said. "I never saw these back here."

"Put it on," he said. "We don't want to have to call your mommy because you got shot."

The weight of that vest wasn't slowing down my heart from beating a hundred miles an hour. The streets were lined with S.W.A.T team sharp shooters. Armed men were squatting near cars, against walls and light posts, taking any cover they could find.

The police allowed us to go surprisingly close, less than a block away. I positioned myself behind our car and got a decent shot of the whole scene. An officer with a megaphone was trying to reason with the man inside, pleading with him to pick up his phone.

The family was in a second floor apartment, and their windows were open. We could hear their phone ringing. The sound seemed to be reverberating off the buildings in the neighborhood, louder and louder. Ten minutes of continual ringing. The man finally poked his head out a window.

"I told you to leave me alone," he yelled. "Now they all pay."

The man stepped back out of sight, and we heard a woman scream, followed by a series of gunshots ringing out through the overcast morning sky. The loud bang of the first shot caught me off guard. I bumped the camera, but I quickly regained my composure. The picture was the vacant window, and the soundtrack was gunfire.

I vividly remember those three seconds after the first shot rang out. There was a slow-motion, or frozen in time feel. All of us who witnessed the sounds of the family's last moments of life were shocked and stunned. Gerald looked at me with a blank look on his face as police and paramedics rushed into the building. I had a hard time concentrating on my job; it was so engrossing and so spontaneous. Instinct and a little luck got me through it.  I took pictures of the constant commotion.

Day quickly turned to night as all the stations began broadcasting the event live. It was a parking lot of news trucks and police cars. My assignment was now to shoot the bodies as they were loaded into the back of police vans (or "meat wagons" as we referred to them). One by one, the officers brought the victims past us. All of them were wrapped in the same green plastic body bags. Other than the clicking of still cameras the entire area was silent as the five victims (three young children, their mother, and the father of the family, who had shot himself as well) were brought out.

A police sergeant approached the TV crews and offered us a chance to videotape one room of the crime scene. I've never seen or heard of such a thing, an opportunity to videotape where these poor people were killed. Before we knew it, we were walking up the stairs of the building. Once we got inside the apartment, we were ushered through the living room into a hallway then told to stay behind the police tape that sealed off the entrance to a bedroom.

The officer standing before us was a lieutenant.

"You'll have exactly two minutes to videotape, then you'll be escorted out of the building," he said. "The children were two boys and one girl, all under the age of thirteen. The room you'll be videotaping belonged to the boys."

There was blood everywhere. The father must have kept them in their room until he decided it was the end. Bloody footprints on the floor lead into another room where he must have then finished off the sister and his wife.

As I panned the camera around the room, I couldn't help but notice that it was a heartbreakingly normal boy's bedroom. There were baseball and basketball trophies, stuffed animals, schoolbooks, and clothes scattered across the room. But this was far from normal. The blood. There was just so much blood. It took my breath away. After we got back outside, the lieutenant held an impromptu press conference explaining what had happened with the family and why he let us in to film the crime scene.

"The father had a history of mental illness," the lieutenant explained. "He had been unemployed for several months, had moved out of the house a couple months before, and came back today with a gun. This guy was a time bomb ready to go off, but therapists and doctors over the years had failed to recognize his condition."

Then the lieutenant hung his head and explained why he had let us see the boy's room.

"I wanted to show the public what we've lost here today. Gone are three children in the prime of their lives, along with their loving mother. Lives taken away by senseless violence. God rest their souls."

I instantly thought "God? Where was God?"

If this is the way we are watched over by a higher power, we're all in deep shit.

*　*　*　*　*

Spring turned to summer. That meant warm weather, which in Chicago meant it was time to deal drugs. Heavily armed inner city kids were selling heroin and coke on the streets.

Gerald and I pulled the short straw. Our assignment was to get video of drug dealers on the southside for an upcoming undercover investigation piece. That entailed a full day of sitting in a van with blacked out windows in the heart of drug dealer land. The only upside to this was we had an armed off-duty cop with us. The downside was that if we were spotted we could get blown away in a heartbeat, cop or not.

We arrived at 6am in one of the city's most violent areas, a section called Englewood. This ten block area had a long history of rape, murder, kidnapping, and drug dealing. Gerald, Officer Don Russell, and I settled in for what turned out to be an extremely long day. The windows of the van were tinted so no one could see us. We sat in uncomfortable folding chairs. Our only comfort was Officer Don's Smith & Wesson.

Don also entertained us by telling us great stories. Don had tales of police shootings, stabbings, bribery, and one about two cops who shot each other in an alley so they could get on disability and retire to their summer homes. Then he told us a story we'll never forget.

"Hey, remember the show *Playtime with Miss Connie*? It was a local TV kids show in the early to mid-1970s."

"Hell yes," I answered. "She was smoking hot."

"I had a thing with her for a couple of years," Don said. "Best I ever had."

Both Gerald and I gasped.

"Bullshit!" Gerald snapped at Don.

"On the head of my children," Don fired back. "She and her husband were good friends with my wife and me. We hung out all the time, but her husband was a sales representative and traveled around a lot. She got lonely. What can I say?"

"That lady was my favorite white chick," Gerald snapped. "I watched her with my son. You were hitting that woman when she was waving her magic wand and wishing kids a happy birthday? Man! Fuck you!"

Gerald was seriously angry. I was troubled by Don's admission. I'm sure Miss Connie was the inspiration for every boy in Illinois getting his first erection. She was a tall brunette, with a striking face and a gorgeous body. Finding out she was sullied by Officer Don left me with a sinking feeling in the pit of my stomach. Don hung his head, realizing he had struck a nerve with us.

Loud hip-hop music broke the strange silence in the van. A group of gang bangers was approaching. Don went into cop mode.

"Be quiet, and stay still," he said.

We were parked half a block away, but the music was so loud it cut right through us as we sat in the van.

I was getting great footage. The gang bangers were dealing crack cocaine. Every now and then, you could see the guns tucked under their jackets as they moved around. We were in the middle of the action getting great video, but we were also becoming surrounded, making it tough for any kind of an exit.

The evening wore on, and it got more crowded and a lot louder. At one point we thought we had caught a break. The party seemingly shifted to another street corner farther away from us. We let out a collective sigh of relief, but thoughts of pulling out of there and leaving came to an abrupt halt when a crack head shuffled over in our direction and decided he'd like to look inside the van.

First he circled us, then he jammed his face right into the

window on the side of the van. The three of us sat motionless for what seemed like an eternity as he circled the van. At one point, it seemed he was about to run out of steam, but then all of a sudden, he backed off and pulled out a gun. Don motioned to us to slowly lay flat on the van's floor while he reached for his gun.

The crack-head was mumbling some bullshit and had an expression of sheer rage on his face. Don still sat in a chair while Gerald and I hugged the floor. Don then calmly pressed his gun barrel to the glass and pointed it right at the drugged out knucklehead.

"I'm going to shoot this asshole next time he points the gun our way," Don whispered to Gerald. "Get behind the wheel when I do and get us out of here."

Gerald nodded.

Don was pointing his gun directly at the crack-head when someone shouted for him to come back and join the group. The man stared at the group for the longest time, then stared back at the van. He slowly tucked his gun back in his pants and walked away. All three of us said the same thing under our breath.

"Oh shit!"

Gerald hopped behind the wheel, but Don made him wait until he thought we were out of range from would-be gunfire. When he got the green light, Gerald hauled ass out of there. Not a word was said until we made it out of the neighborhood and onto the expressway. Don shook his head and sighed.

"That was way too close."

Gerald was still upset.

"I can't believe you banged Miss Connie. You're going to hell, you know."

*　*　*　*　*

One day I was assigned to go to the headquarters of the well-known El Rukns street gang in Chicago, the New York Yankees of gang bangers. Every major gang in the city and suburbs was scheduled to arrive for what was being called a "gang summit meeting." There had been a rash of killings, and the El Rukns decided to take charge and talk to all the leaders of the various factions about stopping the violence.

Imagine how underfunded I felt watching these guys get out of their Lincoln Town Cars, BMWs, Porches, and every other luxury car you can name. They were dressed to the nines and wearing the finest jewelry and the best clothes money can buy.

My partner that day was Willie Samuels. Willie was a legend at our station, not so much for his talent as a cameraman but for being a ballsy and extremely humorous man. Willie took no shit, and he could disarm you with his wit and charm. Willie was a staff cameraman, which meant I was assigned to be audio man for the day.

On that day, I had this feeling in the pit of my stomach that something was a little off-kilter. After I looked at all the other television crews, it finally hit me what was wrong. I was the only white member of the media. Every station in town, even the PBS station, had sent all black crews. Normally I wouldn't have thought twice of such a thing, but every gang member that had gone into this meeting was either black or Hispanic.

"Do you feel like Custer at Little Big Horn?" Willie asked with a smirk.

As every gang leader passed, Willie gave them a nod or a

smile and complimented their cars or clothes. A short Hispanic man piled out of a Lincoln with three other tough looking members of the "Insane Unknowns."

"Nice ride, man," Willie said.

The man stopped and extended his hand.

"I'm V," he said.

Willie set his camera down and shook V's hand.

"Willie Samuels, NBC. This is my partner Chuck. You guys are the best dressed crew so far."

That garnered a huge smile for Willie and me. As "V" walked by, I noticed the FBI agents who had been staked out all day across the street were snapping pictures like crazy. I'm sure Willie and I ended up on a bulletin board somewhere in the federal building with our newfound pal "V".

Finally, a giant black man with some kind of silly-ass fur hat on his head emerged from the inside of their headquarters. He walked over to our reporter Robert and whispered something into his ear. Robert nodded to him then headed toward Willie and me.

"They wanted to know if we'd like to come inside," Robert said. "But if we do, they need to strip search us."

Willie looked at me, then got right in Robert's face.

"Fuck that, man," Willie said. "I'm not doing it. If they want our coverage, then we go in with no strip search."

Willie then walked over to the other television crews, talked to them for about a minute, and then came back to us.

"Tell those assholes that if they want coverage, there won't be any strip searches."

Now, I didn't know Willie all that well, but I instantly gained respect for him. Willie didn't really feel it made much sense that convicted criminals had the right to pat us down since they didn't pat themselves down. He was either a total badass, or he knew nothing would happen because there were federal agents across the street. Either way Robert came out of the building five minutes later and said we could go in with no type of search whatsoever.

We could barely move inside that room. It was assholes to elbows with every gang leader from every major gang in the area. They let us set up our cameras and microphones in the middle of the room. As I put my microphone on top of a podium they had set up for us, I noticed a giant wooden throne behind it. Now, when I say giant, I mean huge. The wood was stained dark brown, and it was covered with medieval-inspired carvings of crowns. I motioned for Willie to come over toward me. I could tell when he saw this thing he was as baffled as me. Willie just shook his head.

"Whatever, man."

After 10 minutes of standing around, the El Rukn members started to chant.

"Rukn love, Rukn love."

That went on for about a minute. Then an older black woman emerged from a back room wearing a long colorful robe. The place went silent. She held her hands extended in front of her as if to bless the crowd, then walked toward the giant throne. It was so quiet you could hear a mouse fart. When she got to the throne, she bowed her head, and a man walked up next to her. He was dressed in a safari outfit and wore a black tam on his head.

"Rukn love, Rukn love," he chanted again.

I looked around the room and noticed some of the other

gang members were quickly tiring of the chanting bullshit. The Hispanic gang members were rolling their eyes, talking to each other, and laughing. If the Rukn guys saw that, they would have been pissed. I worried that a shootout was about to take place.

After the chanting, Safari-man spoke.

"This is Jeff Fort's mother, and she brings us a message from her son."

Jeff Fort was the El Rukn leader convicted of drug trafficking and conspiring with Libya to cause domestic terrorism. That move got him an 80-year stretch. You could tell Mom was anxious to speak. Her outstretched arms commanded silence.

"We are only hurting our future and killing off the next generation," she said, conveying the message she had received from her son.

Everyone in the room seemed to be taking this seriously. As the speech went on, I realized the real reason. Killing was bad for business. As long as the cops were in the hood, it was tough to sell the guns, drugs, and whatever else they sold. If they stopped the killing, business would pick up again.

Mom's speech dragged on and on, and her voice was fading, so I bent down to turn up my audio mixer to hear her better. With the room almost silent, Willie suddenly spoke up in a loud booming voice.

"Did you call me a nigger?" he said.

I looked up to see who he was talking to. He was staring right at me! I was stunned, almost paralyzed. I felt that warm feeling like I was going to piss myself. I slowly started to stand up, looking at Willie the whole time. He spoke up again, in that same agitated tone.

"Don't talk that shit to me, you white motherfucker, did

you call me a nigger?"

I looked to my right, and there were about ten guys looking at me. I turned back at Willie.

"Man, what are you doing to me?" I said.

With that, his stern look went away, and he started to laugh. So did every other guy within a thirty-foot radius. They all laughed really hard.

"Got your white ass!" Willie said.

One of the gang members from a Hispanic gang put his hand on my shoulder.

"Tell your bosses to learn the city," he said. "This is no place for the white man to be today, no offense."

"None taken," I said.

Willie scared the living shit out of me, but I wasn't really mad. He got me good. When the meeting ended we packed our gear and headed out the front door. As Willie and I got close to the crew car he stopped me.

"Hey, man. Look, didn't mean to scare you like that, just fucking with you. No hard feelings?"

He held out his hand. I grabbed his hand and shook it.

"You know I will get even someday." I said.

Willie smiled as he opened the trunk of the car.

"You know," he said, "I'll bet some of those Italian fellows you grew up with in that small town would have shit themselves if they were in that situation. How do you think they would have handled it? You held up pretty good."

I wondered about that the rest of that day. How would some of the guys I knew in my younger days have handled that? In that small town there weren't any gangs. We were mostly Italian kids whose parents were born and raised in that town. The guys who stayed behind and didn't go to college took factory and construction jobs.

I think any one of those guys would have given anything they had to be in that gang headquarters on that day. I felt damn good about the way my life was going. I was working for one of the most powerful news organizations in the world. This job was something different every day. In this case I had just met a whole group of killers who wanted to blow my balls off.

But at least I wasn't doing manual labor.

## Chapter

# LIFE, DEATH AND SWINGERS

NBC was located on the nineteenth floor of the Merchandise Mart building along the Chicago River. The Mart consisted of floors and floors of mini storefronts for furniture and clothing designers and was always packed with hot women and gay men. There were restaurants in the building, along with a few pubs we would all would frequent when our shift was over.

The crew room was located in the building's loading dock, the same area that housed our equipment and cars. That's where we hung out as we awaited the nineteenth floor newsroom call to tell us about our assignment for that day. After the call, out the loading dock we would go. It seemed so well organized.

I had been there a few months when rumors started circulating that only five people would become full-time out of the ninety-five people they had hired on a vacation relief basis.

Talk about pressure.

The four other vacation relief guys in my department were very talented and wanted the gig just as badly as I did. This was my first glimpse of politics in the work place. Not only did you have to do a good job all time, you had to blow your own horn and let the bosses know how well you were doing. Luckily for me, I got along very well with the older guys, and they took me under their wing. They gave me little tips on lighting or framing or just simple politics.

"You should be friendly with everyone at the station," they liked to say, "because you never know who your next boss will be."

One of the guys I got paired up with for a while was Peter Nichols. He had been at NBC for years, ever since he graduated from high school. He started out as a lighting guy but taught himself to shoot. To this day, he's one of the best cameramen the city has ever seen.

Peter was quiet until you got to know him, but once he opened up, he could be extremely funny. He was also the master of politics. He knew every move and was one my biggest supporters, which was a big feather in my cap. After each assignment, Peter would tell the bosses how well I did and would encourage the reporters we worked with to do the same thing.

One day we got the call to meet Gary Monroe, a rookie reporter we had recently recruited from Iowa. We were going to do a story about a girl who needed a new kidney. As we brought the car around the front of the building, I could tell Peter wasn't himself.

"What's up?" I asked.

Peter shook his head. "You've never worked with this asshole before, have you?"

"No," I replied.

"For a new guy, he's a know it all, plus he's really in his own world, mentally. His interviews are way too long because he doesn't know what he wants."

Just as he finished telling me this, Gary hopped in the back of the car and off we went. On our way, Gary was making small talk about some useless bullshit, and I could see Peter smirking.

Peter kept looking in the rearview mirror, then looking at me and then again into the mirror. This was very strange behavior on my friend's part. I really couldn't imagine anyone being as bad as Peter made this guy out to be.

We finally pulled up to the house.

"We're interviewing a sixteen-year-old girl who needs a kidney transplant," Gary said. "Time is running out for her."

Peter and I got our gear from the trunk while our hotshot reporter friend checked his hair in the reflection of the car window. He straightened his tie and cleared his throat as he walked toward the house.

"This should be good," he said. "Guaranteed emotion. Compelling stuff."

Peter looked at me and mouthed the word "Asshole."

Once we were in the house Peter and I were taken downstairs by the girl's father. We set up lights and got everything ready. After a few minutes Gary came down followed by the girl and her mother. She was a normal looking girl, in a beautiful dress with her hair done very nicely. Her mother sat next to her. Mom was a very stately looking woman, her daughter's moral support.

From the moment 16-year-old Laurie opened her mouth, our hearts went into our stomachs. She told of the endless treatments, the pain, and how all of her friends just didn't seem to come around anymore. As she answered each one of the questions that Gary asked her, she took a deep breath to compose herself then with a calm and eloquent manner described every detail about the illness.

We were about twenty minutes into the interview when I pulled my head from the camera and scanned the room. The father was off in the corner, out of camera range and hanging on his daughter's every word. The mother was sitting next to the girl holding her hand. On one of her wrists, a bracelet prominently displayed the word, "HOPE." She appeared very strong, and her presence seemed very reassuring for her daughter.

It wasn't until that moment when I noticed the girl's skin tone was slightly yellow. She later explained it was caused by chronic dehydration and a buildup of calcium deposits in the skin. Her organs were slowing down. We couldn't help feeling sorry for her and admiring her bravery. She wasn't going down without a fight.

Then it happened.

"What happens if you don't get a kidney?" Gary asked.

The girl froze; her mother hung her head, I saw dad turn away.

"I'll die," she whispered, "I'll die."

She started to well up, and a tear streamed down her cheek. Now, rule one for a cameraman is to capture the moment. Zoom in tight. Catch the tears. Gary had just gotten his emotion.

"I'm number seven on the donor list," the girl continued, "but if I don't get one in six months, I'll be in big trouble."

With that, he asked her again. "What happens if you don't get the kidney?"

This time she burst into tears and buried her head in her hands. I couldn't believe it. I pulled the shot back. It was now a two shot, meaning I zoomed back to show her and the back of the reporter. I made sure not to capture her tears this time. I glanced again over at Peter. He looked pissed but flashed me a smile because he knew what I did. Even Gary sensed he may

85

have crossed the line.

"Hopefully this story will give more people the inspiration to become organ donors,
 he said, "to come to the aid of people like you."

The girl regained her composure. She smiled at him, but you could read her mind. She thought our reporter was a total asshole. The interview should have wrapped at this point, but he kept asking the same questions over and over. The girl was tired, her father was pissed, and her mom was scared for her daughter. Peter was right. This clown was way over his head. He had no idea what he's doing. Then he asked her again.

"What happens if you don't get a kidney?"

I couldn't get my hands on the zoom button quick enough. I made the shot as wide as humanly possible. That asshole may have wanted emotion, but wasn't going to get it on that shot. The framing was so wide that her face couldn't even be made out. That's when Laurie's father jumped into the picture and stopped the whole thing.

"Enough is enough," he shouted. "We are done here."

Gary said his goodbyes and went to the car while Peter and I packed up our gear. Peter walked up to the girl and apologized.

"Please don't think of us in the same vein as that goof. We aren't like that. We wish you nothing but the best."

The girl gave both of us a hug and thanked us for coming. Her parents just smiled as we left. They knew. When we got outside, I thought Peter was going to come unglued. I put the gear in the trunk while he walked away from the car and had a cigarette. It took him a while to cool off, but when he finally got in the car he seemed relaxed.

The ride back was silent. When we got close to downtown, Gary leaned forward.

"Chuck, when she started to cry were you on a tight shot?"

I looked at Peter, and he turned his head, looking out the window.

"I was on the first one," I replied. "The second and third one I went as wide as humanly possible."

He was stunned.

"Wide? Why wide?"

Now I was pissed.

"Three fucking times you asked the same question. Did you really need to scare her like that? The kid is fighting for her life, and you want tears for some bullshit news piece?"

Gary leaned back from us to his seat and didn't say another word. I knew it wasn't smart popping off like that, but I just couldn't keep my mouth shut. Peter was smiling as we pulled into the front of the station. Gary got out and slammed the car door. Peter put the car in park and looked at me.

"He's going to go to our bosses and complain. You're part-time, and if you ever want to be full-time you don't need a rap like this in your file. When we get called in, don't say a word. I'll do all the talking."

Sure as shit, ten minutes later we get summoned to the news director's office. As Peter and I were heading in, Gary was walking out. He didn't make any eye contact with us. I sat in the chair that was offered to me, and it started to sink in that I really could get in a world of trouble for this.

The news director was a wiry, fast-talking guy. A little fellow named Dick. He was known for using terms like "dude" and "cool" all the time, which sounded somewhat strange coming out his 50-something mouth. He politely asked me what happened in the field to get our intrepid reporter so upset. As I opened my mouth to form the first word Peter burst in.

"He did only what I told him to do," Peter said. "I'm senior man on this crew, and this falls on me."

The news director seemed taken aback. Peter pressed on, pointing at the door Gary had just departed.

"That man represents the station. He should have had some class and dignity. Instead, he put the full court press on to make a sixteen-year-old girl who's going to die of kidney failure cry. Not once, but three times. I told Chuck to widen his shot the second and third time he asked her the same question, and he did it. At what point do we show compassion? I ask you Dick, at what point?"

Peter voice was dripping with passion.

"Altering his shot may seem silly to you," he continued. "But maybe next time Gary will think twice and remember that crews had fucked him once before, and he'll worry that we'll do it again if he pulls this shit. Ask a question like that once maybe, but not three times. It was way over the line."

The news director fell back in his chair and shook his head.

"He came in here screaming like a maniac," Dick said. "But he sure didn't tell me this. What was the question?"

"What happens if you don't get a kidney?" I answered.

"Painfully obvious what would happen," Dick replied, shaking his head. "Jesus Christ, the shit I deal with on a daily basis."

Peter and I got out of our seats and headed for the door.

"Let's keep this here, guys," Dick said. "I'll talk to him. Please keep it low key."

We nodded. Then, of course, we proceeded to tell everybody who would listen to us.

Four months later I was sitting in the shop watching television and Peter dropped a newspaper in my lap. I glanced down and saw the girl's picture in the obituaries. Time had run out. Her condition had advanced, and she never received a kidney. I thought of her and her parents. I remembered how they hung on her every word. I thought about how devastated they must have been and all the pain they had gone through. I thought of the mother's bracelet and the word "HOPE" and how she hung all her faith on that one word.

We bounce in and out of so many lives in this job and never think twice about the majority of the people we encounter. This one was different. This one stung. This one will stick with me forever.

\* \* \* \* \*

The longer I was at NBC, the more I became absorbed in the atmosphere there. This was a group of people who really wanted to be the best. We were collectively driven to be the number one station in town. The ABC station had been number one in town for years, and now it was our turn. We all felt that way. Overtime was not an issue. No matter what it cost to cover a story, the price was paid.

Everything was clicking on all cylinders until we missed a story one day, a fire on the north side. They called a newsroom meeting to address the problem. The news director had it catered. If you were off the clock, they even authorized the overtime to attend. The allure of free food and time and a half assured our full attendance.

The news director Dick spoke first.

"As a station, we are making a move to be number one," he said. "Now is the time to come together as a group. The better the station does, the better we all do, so let's work together."

The speech did very little to move the surly group. We were running out of finger food and interest. Bob Manning, the main anchor and probably the best anchor the city has ever seen, stood next, and the crowd became silent.

"I've been talking to some of my colleagues, and I think we have a solution to our problem," he said. "One person, one job. The other day with the fire, too many people were involved, one crew was given three different addresses, none of them the right one. I propose that everyone wear a baseball hat with the name of their function on it. For example, Joe the desk assistant will have 'Calling the police' on his hat. Sandy will have 'Calling the fire department' on her hat, and so on."

At first that suggestion was greeted by silence. The quiet was disturbed by a loud bellowing voice.

"Man, that's stupid," Willie Samuels said, after swallowing his fifth hot dog in a croissant. "Fucking baseball hats? That's the best you've got? How about we act like adults and do our fucking jobs? If we screwed up as much out there as you clowns do back here at the station, we'd be fired. But no! When you fuck up, we have a catered meeting." Willie walked toward the exit, stopped, shook his head, turned around and gave us a parting shot. "Our million dollar anchor wants ball hats. How did we ever survive before ball hats?"

The room fell silent.

Bob sat down and stared at the floor. One by one we all got up and filed out of the room, grabbing the remaining food on our way out. That was our last catered meeting ever. Fucking baseball hats.

*　*　*　*　*

By September of 1984, they had run me into the ground. The scheduling department gave me (and the other temporary guys) the old shifting shifts routine. One day I worked 6 am to 2pm, then the next day 3pm to 11pm, then back to 6 am and so on. It was a test to see who would gripe and moan and who would nut up and handle it. I did a fair amount of complaining alone in the privacy of my own home but never to anyone at work.

Rumors were running rampant again that the station was going to hire five of the vacation relief people permanently before the end of the month. I had this unjustified feeling of confidence that I would make it.

One day I was called to Rick Harvey's office. I hadn't seen much of Rick because he made sure to stay clear of us part-time people. He let us walk on our own. I also hadn't seen much of his secretary Nicole (a.k.a. "Barracuda"), but she was very good to me when I did.

One day Rick sat me down and told me he'd like me to travel on the last leg of the Chicago Cubs playoff quest. The Cubbies were expected to clinch the division title on the road, and the station wanted to be there in full force. They were sending six people; four cameramen and two reporters. I jumped at the chance.

As I left his office, Nicole pulled me aside.

"This is good for you," she whispered in my ear. "They

never send vacation relief people on the road. You'll be traveling with all staff people. It's just a matter of time before they make you staff."

 I'm sure I looked like some kind of spastic fool. I gave her a big hug and grinned all the way down the hallway.

First stop was St. Louis, where the Cubs had to win three games to clinch the title. I remember standing on the field before the first game. It was 104° on the field. We were stationed on the edge of the dugout all game in the blazing sun; Willie, myself and reporter Sam Raymond. Our assignment was covering the Cub fans following the team on the road. The other guys traveling with us were covering the sports angle. We never really saw too much of them.

Before the game Willie, Sam and I roamed the streets of St. Louis looking for Cub fans showing their pride for the team. Unfortunately, all we found was a pack of drunken knuckleheads who called in sick from their jobs so they could go to a different city and make assholes out of themselves. Once the game started, we baked to death in the sun and tried to photograph the damn-near comatose Cub fans in the stands. That sun really drained us, but by the grace of God we managed to make it through the game, and muster the strength to hit the bars that night.

That night at the hotel bar, a half-in-the-bag suburban housewife mistook Willie for a Cub player whose name I won't mention. She was all over him. She pointed out her husband across the bar, waving like a two-year-old kid in our direction. She said they were lifelong Cub fans from a Chicago suburb and wanted to know if Willie was open-minded.

Willie nodded his head yes. The woman then put her hand

on Willie's crotch and asked if he'd like to have sex with her while her husband watched. Willie smiled.

"I don't do anything without my road roommate," he said, pointing to me and introducing me as a pitcher on the team. I did kind of look like the pitcher Willie mentioned. With that the woman let out a shriek, gave me a hug, and started pointing across the room where that freak she was married to was sitting.

Willie leaned in close to her. "Go ask your husband if he'd like us both to do you."

The woman's eyes got big as saucers.

"Really?" she asked.

"Really," he said.

She nearly sprinted across the room to share the news with her weirdo husband.

"Have you lost your mind?" I asked. "That's not happening."

"I know. She's a dog, right?"

"Dog or not. With her husband watching?"

"Just wanted to see how far she'd go," Willie said, laughing. "She really went for it, too. The hubby's a freak who likes to watch his wife get banged. Shit, now what?"

"I don't know," I replied, "but you better think of something. She's coming back with him."

With that Willie pushed me toward the door, and out of the bar we went.

The next day at the game, I was discretely looking into the stands to see if I could spot the couple. I never did. Willie and I would laugh every time that certain ballplayer came to bat. It was stupid fun.

Our last night in St. Louis, we went to a piano bar. After six gin & tonics, Sam turned in a blistering version of "My Way" followed by a first time ever piano version of "Johnny B. Goode." The crowd of nine people in the pub cheered wildly as Sam took a drunken bow before falling to one knee. We laughed so hard we cried. Willie and I jumped on stage and whisked our drunken buddy into the rental car and back to the hotel.

The Cubs couldn't clinch in St. Louis, so we had to stay with them until they clinched the division in the next city. Our next stop was Pittsburgh. The Cubs needed only one win, and we could all go home. We had only been on the road four days but the combination of heat, lack of sleep, excessive alcohol, and fatty foods were starting to take a heavy toll on us. Luckily, the first game was all they needed. The Cubs took the Pirates easily 4-1.

There were only a few thousand fans in the stadium. Most of them were crazed Cub fans that had followed these guys like Grateful Dead fans. The celebration was low key, at least in the stadium.

Back in Chicago, the city was up for grabs. Willie and I stood in the outfield of Pirate stadium watching the scoreboard showing the celebrations back in Chicago. There were fights, cars were being overturned, fires, you name it. Our colleagues back home were really having a hard time. It seemed very dangerous. We were happy to be where we were.

In the locker room the champagne was flying and we were soaked, but it didn't matter. Famous announcer Jack Brickhouse interviewed the players in the locker room on WGN-TV, the station that carried the game. That was a strange sight because

Brickhouse was retired at the time. Harry Caray was the play-by-play guy, but he was nowhere to be found.

We were videotaping the celebration and purposely getting in the shots behind Brickhouse so the folks back home could see us. After we got what we needed, Willie and I slipped off into the corner of the locker room. That's when we saw him—Harry Caray, all alone, sitting on a stool. We nodded, and he smiled. He raised a can of Budweiser in our direction. I remember his lips. They were fleshy, meaty, wet, and shiny, one of those weird things that catches your eye.

As things wound down, the Cubs public relations guy said they were all going to a bar in downtown Pittsburgh, and the Chicago media was invited. We had had enough of the locker room, so we exited the stadium and headed to our hotel to change and put our equipment away. We were really high-rolling it on that trip, rooms on the club floor of a Holiday Inn downtown. After I came back down to the lobby, my buddies were waiting for me like a couple of hopped up crack heads.

"You're not going to believe who is passed out right here in the lobby," Sam whispered.

"It's Harry Caray," Willie chimed in. "Come look."

We crept toward the aging broadcaster slowly. He was sitting upright with his eyes closed with not a soul around. We stood there and stared, like the three wise men staring at the baby Jesus in his manger. Sam took a couple of steps closer.

"Harry, hey Harry," he whispered.

With that, his head shot back, and his eyes opened wide.

"Hey fellas!" he shouted. He was alive and well.

"Harry, we're going to that bar for the celebration. Want a ride?" Sam asked.

Harry rose up from the chair and shot us a huge smile.

"Hell yes," he replied.

We had rented a Lincoln Town car, and Willie was driving. I was in front, and Sam and Harry got in back. We just let Harry be, and he gazed out the window. I pulled the visor down multiple times on the passenger side and glanced back at those wet shiny lips highlighted by the glow from the streetlights. He sure was an odd-looking guy.

When we got inside the crowded pub, we found a table. Harry bought a round of beers, stood up, studied each one of our faces, smiled, and excused himself.

We never saw him again that evening.

It was around 2am when we decided to leave. We were over-served and tired, and we had an 8am flight back to Chicago. But as we weaved our way to the front door, we saw a sight that stopped us dead in our tracks.

The swinger couple we had met in St. Louis was sitting at a table with a ballplayer, the same player they had mistaken Willie for in that hotel bar. She had her hand on the player's leg, and her husband was smiling ear to ear. Willie turned to me and shook his head.

"Let's get home," he said. "I've had enough of this crazy shit."

# Chapter

## A MADE MAN AND THE BIG CITY

The word came down in the form of a note tacked to a bulletin board in the crew room. I was being summoned to the chief engineer's office. He was the main man, the dictator of my fate.

The elevator doors clanged open, and I entered the lobby. The big NBC logo that hung over the television monitors on the wall caught my eye. There was the hustle and bustle of people up and down the hallways. I loved that atmosphere, and I realized that no matter what was going happen, it had been a great experience.

I had just come back from the Cubs clincher, and even though I had showered in Pittsburgh, I smelled and felt like a turd. If someone were to follow me as I walked down that long hallway, they would have been engulfed in a cloud of filth just like Pig Pen's cloud in the Peanuts cartoons. As I rounded the corner and headed into the chief engineer's office, my head and heart were racing. I never wanted anything as much as I wanted this job.

I strolled past the secretary who waved me into the office. I tapped on the half-opened door, and there he was sitting at his desk: Jim Peters, the man who held my future in his hands.

"Hello Chuck," he said. After a firm handshake, he

smiled. "Have a seat. I've got good news. We've been keeping an eye on you, and you've been doing a great job for us. We'd like to offer you a staff job."

Just then, Rick Harvey walked in and shook my hand.

"Welcome aboard," he said. "Good to have you here full-time."

I was overwhelmed. Jim came around the desk and put his hand on my shoulder.

"You've got a job for life," he whispered.

A job for life! That was an awfully bold statement. It was a guarantee with no real backing, but I took it. As I was leaving the room, Rick had a strange look on his face. I figured it was probably the funk trail that I was leaving behind.

Down in the shop most of the guys were waiting. One by one they congratulated me. Two other guys made it in our department, and two more in another. Willie walked up to me and stared directly into my eyes. He put his hands on both my shoulders.

"Your last name is too hard to pronounce. From now on you are Q! Got it?"

A staff job that was accompanied by an official nickname; I had made it.

I nodded to a smattering of applause.

\* \* \* \* \*

My first apartment was in Oak Park, a suburb just west of the Chicago City limits. Between my neighborhood and down-town I had to travel through the west side—a really tough part of town.

I would laugh on my daily "L" train commute, watching the faces of the white suburbanites. They sat nervously as the trains rumbled through the heart of the west side of the city. It reminded me of the characters in the movie Jurassic Park. The people marveled at the dinosaurs as they traveled via tram around the park, but when they stopped or exited, they were scared shitless.

My hours were eight to four. Normally, I would leave right on time, but even if I worked a little overtime, I still had some daylight on my journey home. One day, Willie and I were sent to a giant fire on the city's South Side. It was in an old abandoned factory that stretched an entire city block, but the fire department feared it could spread.

Willie and I were in a live truck. We spent our entire day and evening at the fire scene doing live shots for every show, and that included the ten o'clock news. By the time we packed up the truck and headed back into the city it was close to midnight. I had taken the train that day. Willie said he would take the truck back to the station and asked if I'd like to be dropped off at the "L" stop.

My friend must have sensed a little apprehension in my voice when I accepted his offer. As we pulled the truck up to the train station, Willie gave me what he thought was the most sound and lifesaving advice anyone could give to another human being.

"Listen man," he said, "you're going to be the only white dude on that train, so the only way you're going to survive is to do two things. You listening?"

"Yes, I am."

"All right, first thing you do is put your butt next to the

conductor. He has a radio; he can call for help if you're getting an ass kicking. Second and most important thing to do is this: if the brothers look at you, stare back at them. Don't you fucking back down; give them the eye till they back down. They'll think your white ass is crazy, and they won't want to mess with you."

"That's your advice for me to survive the ride home? Stare down the brothers?"

"You're a man now, Weedhopper," Willie said smiling. "Leave me."

With that, he sped away.

As I climbed the stairs to the train platform, I was more tired than afraid. I was just too tired to care about my impending doom. I was the only one standing on the platform. A couple of bums were asleep on the benches. After a short wait, a two-car train with the conductor in the second train stopped in front of me. There were plenty of seats in the first car. The second car was standing room only. Based on my streetwise friend's advice, I shoe-horned myself into car number two right before the doors closed. Did I forget to mention that I was the only white person on both cars?

The first couple of stops were a blur. I kept my head down, making eye contact with no one. People filed out at every stop. As they did, I inched closer to the conductor. Half way through my journey I finally made it right next to my guardian angel. I lifted my head to look around for the first time, and I saw several hostile looks aimed at me. I looked in the conductor's direction to find a little compassion.

I received nothing.

The one man that was supposed to be my savior, my protector was giving me the same "Fuck off look" as the rest of the train. My eyes went to the floor again. As we pulled up to the Central Avenue stop, the doors opened up, and no one was there. We sat there for a second, when we suddenly heard screams from out of nowhere. An older black man came flying up the stairs to the platform covered in blood.

"Please wait! Please. They are going to kill me!"

The conductor reached up, hit the switch, and the doors closed before the man could get in. That stunned the shit out of me. I looked over at the conductor. Now he was the one with his head down. As the train pulled away I saw the man who was left behind just getting an ass-kicking by what looked to be three younger men.

I couldn't believe what I had just witnessed. The conductor didn't even use his radio to call the police for that guy. For all I knew, the man got killed that night. Not a word was said by anyone. There was no emotion at all from anyone on the train.

The train kept getting closer to my destination. Even though I realized Willie's first theory was bullshit, I decided to put theory number two into action. There were two guys on the train that had been giving me the evil eye the entire time. I decided to go for broke. At first I looked off in the distance, then I just glared right back at them. This went on for at least five minutes. Two stops, three stops, I was locked on to them and they me. It started to seem a little like a game you'd play when you were a little kid, but then I realized these weren't little kids and they could probably gut me like a deer if they wanted.

There were only two stops left until I was home. As we eased into the next stop, the two men stood up; still staring. The train to came to a complete stop, and one of the men reached into his jacket pocket.

"Uh oh," I said to myself.

This was how it would end for me; blown away on an "L" train. But then he smiled and handed me a card. I looked at the card.

"Sonny and Jerry: Singers, comedians and caterers."

* * * * *

## A SNAPSHOT IN TIME/ JANUARY 1986/SUPER BOWL XX

A week before they went to New Orleans for the big game the Bears spent a week in Champaign, Illinois practicing under a dome. They were rock stars. Everywhere they went people followed in droves. We were in a hotel suite doing an interview with William "Refrigerator" Perry when all of a sudden two heads popped up in the hotel window smiling and yelling, "Fridge, Fridge!" We were on the third floor.

The night shift was a consistent source of entertainment. Close to the end of our shift, the night truck operator, Bill, and I got a call to check out a murder on the city's far west side. It was a hot summer night, and people in this neighborhood were killing each other on a nightly basis. The murders had become so frequent that the desk didn't show too much interest if the story made the show or not. They just wanted us to check it out in case it turned into something big.

We were piloting a four-wheeled billboard: a two-hundred and fifty thousand dollar live truck with NBC painted in bright colors on both sides of the vehicle, announcing to everyone carrying a weapon that two boneheads were on their way.

We quickly figured out that no matter how big a story this was, we weren't going to be staying long. The murder occurred at the end of a one-way street. The area was congested with police cars and people who must have figured whoever was dead at the end of the block was more interesting than whatever else they were doing that evening. Bill looked at me.

"Now what?" he wondered aloud.

We knew we would never get the truck through all the people and make it to the scene, so I volunteered to get out and walk. Bill gave me a "nice knowing you" look, and off I went. I walked through the crowd of curious onlookers, and made a bee-line for the first police officer I found. My new best friend was a captain and the only white officer on duty. He put his hand on my shoulder and whispered in my ear.

"You and your buddy should make this quick. We're the only pale faces within a fifteen mile radius. Come with me. It's a murder, and we have the killer."

The captain parted the crowd to reveal the murder victim. Lying down on the front stairs of his home was a sixty-something year old man. His eyes were wide open, and he had a meat clever jammed nicely in the center of his chest. The captain explained that this guy had been running around on his wife, and she found out about it. She had waited for him in the bushes and when he came home, that was all she wrote.

"See his eyes?" the captain asked. "They are wide open. My guess is she really surprised the shit out of him."

"This is a domestic, and we don't cover domestics," I said. "I think we should be leaving now".

"Very smart. If you were to bring out that camera, we'd be in a world of shit."

We nodded to each other, and I walked back. Weaving through the crowd, I came upon a squad car. In the backseat, I saw an older woman in handcuffs. Our eyes met, and she quickly lowered her head. She probably was someone's grandmother, but now she was going do a stretch for murder.

As I got closer to the truck, I could hear Bill shouting at the crowd assembling around him.

"What do you mean what channel are we with? Can't you read? It's all over the truck. What's wrong with you?"

I got in the passenger side of the truck.

"Are you trying to get us killed?" I whispered.

We started our trek back, but we were diverted off the main roads due to construction. We were already in unfamiliar territory, but now we were really confused.

"If we just go east," Bill said, "We may get shot, but at least we're heading in the right direc—"

Bill was in mid-sentence when he suddenly slammed on the brakes sending me into the dashboard of the truck and almost through the windshield. Bill's mouth was wide open. We were bathed in neon light. Bill groaned and pointed upward.

We were the middle of one of the worst neighborhoods in the city, but we had found Mecca. I had never seen such a thing. The glow from the neon beacon was a call to all that would answer. It was a bar that stretched almost a city block long. The neon light that shown brightly that evening displayed the greatest bar name ever: Tits Lounge.

Bill and I sat in silence paying homage to something we previously had no idea existed. We had a real dilemma on our hands. How could we get so close to a place called 'Tits' without going in? Bill was adamant about taking a chance.

"Look," I said, "As much as I'd like to see it too, we'll never get out of there alive. Is it really worth dying for?"

Bill didn't go down without a fight.

"Do you think they sell T-shirts?" he asked.

A 'Tits Lounge' T-shirt would have made a fine addition to my upscale line of clothing, so I struck a deal with Bill.

"I swear to you," I said, "I will call this place first chance I get, and I'll order us some shirts. Hell, if they have them, I'll even come back in the daytime and pick them up."

Bill reluctantly agreed.

I called the lounge repeatedly with no answer. About a month later when I finally got through to someone, a gruff voice on the other end simply told me the score.

"We don't sell any fucking shirts."

\* \* \* \* \*

One day, Gerald and I were sitting in our crew car when we got the call that we'd be working with Cindy Young, anchorwoman, reporter, and God's gift to journalism. When I asked where we were going with her highness, the desk person told me that we'd be informed when she and her producer arrived. Cindy always traveled with a producer named Tammy. This chick was a nasty looking broad who thought she was hot.

"Speak only when spoken to," Gerald advised. He hoped we wouldn't have to spend too much time with them. These chicks were famous for running to management if something wasn't done to their satisfaction.

They piled into the backseat and talked amongst themselves, without even acknowledging that Gerald and I were in the car. We had no idea where we were going or what we were doing. We just stayed parked.

They eventually realized we weren't going anywhere, so producer Tammy leaned into the front seat and curtly barked out her orders.

"Head to Cicero."

"Where in Cicero?" Gerald asked.

"Just head that way, please," Tammy replied.

Cicero is a town on the Chicago border that has been plagued with corruption since its inception. We headed on the Eisenhower expressway toward our destination. As time passed, I spun around in the front seat and looked right at her majesty.

"Cindy, what exactly is our story? Who are we after today?"

She threw me the most spiteful look I've ever seen anyone give to another human being.

"We'll let you know when we get there," Tammy replied for her.

That was followed by a very unsettling silence. Feeling emasculated, I slowly turned my body around and slid back into the front seat.

"Remember," Gerald whispered, "Speak only when you're spoken to."

Tammy finally gave us the address of a long time suspected head of one of Chicago's crime families, after we entered Cicero's city limits. We slowly crawled down a side street and parked half a block away from a huge house. A fat guy was washing his car with two goons standing around him.

The two in the back seat were all excited, especially Cindy. I really thought she was close to orgasm. She broke her "no talking to other human beings" rule and grabbed my arm.

"We're going up rolling," she said. "Stay with me, and whatever you do, don't shut off the camera!"

She threw the back door open and ran out while Tammy stayed seated in the back of the car. Gerald looked at me, and we both just started laughing. What the hell was going on? We grabbed our gear and followed her. As I turned the camera on, I realized Cindy was a good 50 feet ahead of us. We literally had to run to catch up as she started her verbal bombardment.

Keeping her in one corner of the frame while keeping the mobster in the rest of the picture was no easy task. She was hopping side to side like an ape while the mobster was circling his car and wiping it off.

To his credit, the mob boss played along, answering three or four questions about other mobsters and political allies. He then stopped, lit a cigar, informed our friend Cindy she was trespassing, and suggested she leave quickly. Cindy kept firing questions at him as the two gorillas protecting the mobster got closer.

Gerald, who had been holding a boom microphone the entire time, grabbed me by the back of my jeans and guided me from the driveway and toward the street, out of harm's way. We were now videotaping from the safety of public property. Wonder Woman decided to push the envelope, staying in the driveway and peppering our mob friend with questions. Knowing no one would lay a hand on her, she peppered him with question after question. I kept rolling the camera in hopes those guys would pull out their guns and blow her ass straight to hell.

After another minute, the mobster got tired of playing the

game with her and went into the house. Cindy turned to us with a crazed smile.

"Did you get all that?" she screamed. "That was great! Just what we were looking for!"

Producer Tammy exited the car and patted Cindy on the back. The ride back was all smiles. There was even some friendly conversation between us mere mortals and the superior beings from a galaxy far faraway. Then it happened. I could hear Cindy whisper something into Tammy's ear. Tammy leaned toward us.

"Did you get a shot of the mobster's ring?" she asked.

"The ring?" I replied. "I didn't notice any ring as we were chasing him around the car."

There was dead silence. I turned to the backseat and looked at both of them. I wanted to continue the conversation but was met with a stern look. When we pulled in front of the station, the two piled out of the car without a word. Tammy almost slammed the back door right off the hinges.

"I didn't hear them say shit about a ring," Gerald said, "so let's get our story straight because these characters are going to cry to the bosses, and we'd better be ready."

"Screw that," I shot back. "We did nothing wrong."

Sure as shit, twenty minutes later both Gerald and I were summoned to meet with the chief engineer, Jim Peters. This was the same man who had given me a staff job just a few weeks earlier.

"Close the door guys," he said. "I just was visited by Tammy, Cindy's shadow. It seems you missed a shot that was critical for their story."

I looked at Gerald and then at Jim.

"I can honestly tell you that I tried to talk to these people before we got to the story about what to look for, but they wouldn't tell me a thing," I said. "Chasing a guy around a car and trying to keep him and Cindy in the frame was somewhat of a feat. How was I supposed to look for a ring I never was informed about? Jim, I've never encountered people like those two. Gerald and I gave our best effort, and they wouldn't even acknowledge our existence. I'm sorry, but their arrogance fucked up their story."

Jim looked at us and smiled.

"Two years ago that woman invited my wife and I to her house for a party she was throwing," he said. "Halfway through the party, she left the room and never returned. She left a room full of people alone in her house. We eventually let ourselves out of her home. I think she's in her own world. Between us, I know you guys gave it your best shot. Don't sweat it."

Gerald and I thanked Jim and left.

We just happened to catch Tammy coming at us down the hallway. No one else was around. Gerald yelled at her.

"Hey, next time you want to tattle, have something on us."

Tammy approached us and shoved her acne-riddled face directly into mine.

"Cindy will never work with you again," she barked.

True to her word, Cindy never did work with me again.

Wherever they are today, I'm sure she and Tammy are still as charming as they were that day in Cicero.

When I was growing up and music was played in my house it was always Tony Bennett. He is an incredible singer and and extremely nice man.

Right before this photo was snapped I moved next to Reggie Jackson to get in frame, he jumped away from me and said "Don't touch me!"

Jay Leno had no problem getting close...notice the goofy look on my face.

Met this happy guy at a cutlery convention.

My first communion, looks like a fun bunch.

My first day of kindergarden, academically my best year, ever...

This picture was taken at the first Cubs-Padres playoff game in 1984. That was about a week or so after our late night meeting in Pittsburgh. From then on Harry Caray always said hello... Had no clue who I was, but always said hello.

Taller than the world's greatest basketball player Michael Jordan only because I had a pompadour.

## Chapter

# AN EDUCATION IN LIFE

At the time, NBC Chicago never flinched when it came to chasing a story. One day, after finishing a shoot, sound man Bob and I received word that we were to head directly to Midway Airport. One of our reporters, Lori Norman, and a producer, were waiting for us there. The four of us boarded a small plane with four passenger seats.

We were heading to a small town near Cincinnati, Ohio, to meet a woman who was being reunited with her two children. Apparently her ex-husband had taken them from the mother and had been on the run for over four years.

The producer gave me an envelope containing five one hundred dollar bills and instructions to call a local woman once we landed because we were renting her family's station wagon for the morning to get to our story. There were no rental cars anywhere nearby, and someone was clever enough to find this housewife who wanted to make some money by renting us her car. We were packed in that airplane like sardines. There was the pilot, copilot, the four of us, and all of our television gear. There was no room to move at all.

Despite the constant up and down motion of the plane, we made it in relatively good spirits. When we landed, I found a pay phone and was dialing the number when I spotted a woman with a ridiculous looking beehive hairdo wearing a housecoat.

"You with NBC?" she snapped at me.

"I am," I replied.

She tossed me a set of car keys and held out her hand. I wasn't sure how much to give her, so I dug in my pocket and pulled out a hundred dollar bill.

"My kids get off school at two o'clock," she said. "I'll be here at one 1:45. You have my number if there is a problem, and there better not be any problems."

The four of us traveled to a town about 25 miles away. The car smelled like a combination of cigarette smoke and ass. The window on the driver side was broken, and the car had no air conditioning, so the 25 miles seemed like an eternity.

Once we got there, we prepared to set up for a press conference given by the reunited woman and her children. It was a large gathering of local Ohio camera crews and reporters. I wasn't really paying attention while I set up my camera.

"Hey asshole," I heard from the side.

It was network cameraman Johnny C. along with his longtime partner, soundman David. Both men were members of the NBC Network Chicago bureau located in the same building as our station. After exchanging pleasantries, we tried to figure the logic of sending two crews from Chicago to cover the same story in Ohio. It was obviously redundant, but what the hell.

"Who is here with you guys?" I asked.

"We're traveling in style with the one and only Mister Huge," David said, smiling broadly.

"Holy shit, not Huge."

Mr. Huge was a network producer who had been with NBC

for many years. Early in his career, Huge and a correspondent did an award-winning series about prostitution. From then on, they had carte blanche to do whatever they wanted to do. Huge treated the crews like champs, always grabbing the tab for dinners, giving them tons of overtime, and always making sure the travel was first class. Huge got his nickname for another reason as well. Huge was Huge. He was an out of shape white dude with ill-fitting clothes. But he had a magnetic personality and a line of bullshit ten miles long. Now, for the first time, I was going to meet the legend.

Huge put his arm around me as soon as he saw me.

"I've heard great things about you," he said. "I have the privilege of working with the greatest cameramen every day, and from what I've been told, you're in that same league." Huge was shoveling the shit hard and fast, and I was hanging on every word. I was wondering what he was going for, what he wanted from me, but it didn't take me long to figure it out.

"Here's my plan, my friend. My crew will shoot all the speaking at the podium. You shoot the cutaways [everything else], and we'll take the footage to Cincinnati, marry everything together, feed it back to Chicago, and everyone will be happy. And by the way buddy, your footage will be on Nightly News. That's as good as it gets."

As Huge walked away, I looked at my reporter Lori. She rolled her eyes.

"I'll call Chicago and tell them the game plan," she said.

David came up to me and smiled. "He's good, isn't he? He just got twice the footage in half the time. Don't worry; he'll take care of you guys. Play along."

So I did. I was all over the room during the press conference getting shots of the woman from different angles. Shots of her kids sheltered in their mother's arms. Shots of the kids while they smiled, cried, and laughed. All of the emotional stuff no one else had the luxury to shoot.

When it ended, Huge approached me with his hand extended.

"I was watching you," he said. "I liked what I saw. This is going to work perfectly." Huge motioned to Lori and her producer. "You guys come with us. I have a limo outside. We'll take that to Cincinnati."

"Now that's the way to travel," I said to Bob.

"What are you going to do about that woman's car?" Bob asked. "We never had Cincinnati in our original plans."

I had totally forgotten I had that woman's car, and we were 25 miles away with no intention of going back. I had limo on the brain, and there was no turning back. I went to Huge for his guidance.

"Call and bribe her," he advised. "Everyone has a price. She let you use it for a price, didn't she? Give her more."

I found her number crumbled up with the hundreds left in my pocket and dialed.

"Hello," she answered.

I explained my predicament, and at first, it was met with silence. That silence didn't last long.

"You son of a bitch," she screamed at me. "I need to pick up my kids from school. For a lousy hundred dollars I have to put up with this shit?"

I was watching Huge and company pile into the limo. Beers were being passed around! Urgency now came into play.

"All right, lady, I get it. Here's the deal; I'll put the keys above the driver side visor and another hundred dollars with it."

"I don't know," she replied.

Now I was losing my mind because Huge was waving a Heineken in my direction.

"All right, two hundred and that's it," I countered.

Ten-seconds of silence followed. I looked at Huge and the Heineken. I looked at the silent phone, then back to Huge.

"Bless you," she finally said.

I gave her the address, put the keys and money in the visor on the driver's side, dove into the limo, grabbed a beer, and headed toward Cincinnati in network style. There was something about traveling the countryside in a limo. I watched the producers working the phones, lining up satellite times. They booked windows for feeding video and hit times for live shots. I was passed another beer, and I couldn't help thinking about my days in Rockford. How did I get to this point? There was no turning back.

When we got to Cincinnati, we were escorted to the roof of a production house with satellite capabilities and a beautiful view of downtown Cincinnati. This is where Lori would do her live shots for our Chicago audience. Huge took all the footage into the facility and fed it to Chicago for us and to New York for the Nightly News.

In true Huge style, right before our live shot, as the sun was setting over the city, full rib dinners and ice-cold Heinekens arrived for everybody. I was on overtime, on a beautiful summer night with the network boys. Seeing how they did things and how they were treated, I thought it really couldn't get any better than this.

We finished our shots back to Chicago, and Huge approached me.

"Just thought you'd like to know, New York loved what we gave them. Your footage made the piece. They loved the emotional shots, great job."

Huge took a couple of steps away from me, then turned around.

"Oh yeah," he added. "Hope you don't mind, but I told my boss and yours what a great job you did. I also took the liberty of sending your plane back to Chicago. Why don't you guys come back with us in the Lear jet?"

I thanked him and accepted his offer. David caught my eye in the distance and smiled. He was right; Huge did take care of me. The plane rose in the darkness and punched through the clouds, catching what was left of the fading sun, and I stared out the window taking in the view and enjoying the silence of the ride. Bob, who was sitting directly across from me, raised his beer bottle and smiled. I reached into my pocket and pulled out the remaining two hundred dollar bills. I handed one to him, and tucked the other one back into my pocket.

"I guess that crazy housewife charged us five hundred dollars," I said with a smile.

\* \* \* \* \*

When I was paired up with Willie, I always enjoyed myself. The shop was packed with good-hearted and fun people, but when it came to having the best time, Willie was the man. Between his stories of the old days and his ability to fit into any crowd or situation, he was my mentor and teacher.

Willie had a cavalier attitude about bullshit things, but he also had a serious side. On one occasion, Willie, reporter Peter O'Donnell, and I were on the North Side of Chicago covering a fire in brutally cold conditions. We were there for almost an hour when word came down that no one was injured, which meant that the show producers didn't really care about this story anymore.

We gravitated to a nearby nursing home for some shelter and a shot at getting warm. The residents and staff welcomed us. Peter was instantly recognized, and everyone seemed to get a kick out of seeing a television camera in the building. It was all older people, mostly women. These people were either mentally together and physically in bad shape, or physically good and mentally gone. It was sad. We watched in silence, as they all filed by us.

Willie, the lone black man, was the favorite with the older women. One by one they would walk by him and touch his face and either smile or laugh. I was talking to a nurse when an elderly man came between Peter and me and whispered to us.

"Can you boys please help me?" he whispered. "I've got to get out of here; I've got to stop her. That bitch is spending all my money. Please help me, boys!"

The nurse put her arm around the man and started to walk him away from us. Willie, who overheard what the man said, questioned the nurse.

"What's his deal? Is he talking about his wife?"

"His name is Sam, and he's been with us along time," the nurse whispered. "His wife passed quite a while ago, and his sons who live out of state put him here, and they rarely if ever visit. We're his family. He's a wonderful man who is actually quite lucid, except when he talks about his wife. He thinks she ran off on him, and it just wasn't the case. Poor guy has no one. I don't think there's a nurse, orderly or a doctor who hasn't given up personal time to bring their families here for a holiday to do something with him to make him feel wanted."

Our new friend, Sam, came strolling back our way holding a handful of one-dollar bills.

"Cheri honey," he said. "I'm taking my new friends across the street for a shot and beer. What do you say, boys?'

"I don't think so Sam," the nurse answered back, "These gentlemen are busy, and they don't have time."

I looked over at Sam, and instead of being disappointed, the kind old man leaned toward the three of us.

"You guys are good friends," he said. "It's been a while since I drank with friends. Let's get loaded and find that bitch!"

The three of us burst into laughter. You had to love this guy. He reminded me of some of the older Italian guys in my hometown. Sam entertained us until the director of the nursing home came out and introduced himself.

"So, what's going on here?" he asked.

"Sam wants us to spring him," Willie said, "so we can go drinking."

Willie and the director stepped into an adjacent office out of earshot and talked a few more minutes. Then both men smiled and shook hands. Willie walked out of the room, and we had no idea where he went until Sam pointed out the window.

"My friend," he yelled, "Look! My friend."

Peter and I went to the window, and saw Willie coming out of the liquor store with a brown paper bag. He strolled past the front desk like he owned the place and right into the lunchroom. We all sat down at a table. Willie passed us each a beer from the six-pack he bought. Sam raised his can, said cheers, and took a long slow drink. He put his left hand on Willie's arm.

"This reminds me of summers in my backyard," he said. "My wife, kids, my brother, and his family. My brother loved beer. He got shot in the leg in the Second World War. Always bothered him, but he never complained. He was always there for me."

Sam took another long swig and seemed to savor this one even more. I looked at the other guys, and they seemed just as mesmerized as I was. Minutes ago, he was just an old man losing his faculties. Now, we were hanging on his every word.

"I didn't go to the war," he explained. "Deaf in one ear, so I stayed behind and worked in the foundry and kept the women company while the boys were gone." He had a sly smile on his face. "Met my Jenny at a local dance. I had the choice of the whole room, and there she was. I never let her go."

Another drink followed and so did the sound of the empty can hitting the table. Willie slid him another beer. Sam never noticed we were drinking non-alcoholic beers.

"I worked hard and raised my boys," he said. "They went to college. You always want your kids to do better. They call and send me money." He took another drink and stared out the window. "Everyone I loved is gone. It's hard some days to face the day."

We looked at each other. That was our cue to leave. As we got up to leave, Sam was still sat staring out the window, deep in thought. Willie stood up and slowly removed his arm from Sam's grip.

"We're friends for life," Sam said, snapping out of his trance. "Come back and visit sometime."

"Yes, please do," Nurse Cheri said. "It was kind of you to hang out here. It seems to have brought back some good memories for Sam."

The old man gave Willie a hug and whispered in his ear. Willie burst into laughter and hugged Sam back. It was an odd ending to our visit. Willie was laughing so hard he had tears in his eyes as we walked out of the building.

"He wanted me to know that the Italians were the only ones that can handle us blacks," Willie explained. "So I better behave."

Laughing again, Willie started the car.

"That's funny shit," he said.

# Chapter

## NASTY PICTURES

When we weren't in live trucks, we traveled in Ford Crown Victorias; they looked like undercover police cars. Willie and I were both big guys, and in those cars we looked like undercover cops. We always parked at a Mrs. Fields Cookies on Rush Street so we could watch women in the summer. When we got hungry, we'd go in there with our radios in hand, which also looked exactly like police radios. We'd order four or five cookies and some milk, and it was always free because they thought we were officers and loved having us around. We made them feel safe.

If only they knew.

In the middle of all the fancy hotels and restaurants, there was one hotel/flophouse that was home to lots of seedy characters. We loved watching them go in and out of the building. One of our favorites was a blonde prostitute who would get out of a Chevy, then moments later get into a limo. This girl was a small corporation, full service 24/7. One day she spotted us from across the street and headed in our direction.

"Howdy," she said with a heavy southern accent.

"Howdy back," Willie responded, not missing a beat. "Where y'all from?"

"I'm from a small town in Alabama," she said.

"Really?" Willie replied. "I'm good friends with Governor

George Wallace."

That went right over her head, but she was smart enough to know we weren't cops, and we were smart enough to know she wasn't selling Amway products.

"What do you boys do?" she asked.

"We're cameramen for a local television station," I said.

"Do you take nasty pictures?" she asked.

A nickname was born.

Every chance we got it was off to Rush Street because the warmer it got, the more skin we saw. We saw Nasty coming or going every single time, and God love her, she would always wave. We were on a first name basis with a prostitute. My mother would be so proud.

One afternoon, when we were in our favorite spot, we received a call telling us to get to the near west side because there had been a shooting. Willie loved driving fast through the neighborhoods, especially if it meant going the wrong way on a one-way street. When we made it to the scene in this Hispanic neighborhood, the streets were lined with at least a hundred people. They were pushing and shoving, trying to see something.

Willie and I approached the scene because we were curious ourselves. In the middle of the now unruly crowd, five Chicago cops were shoving people away from a parked car. We could see the blood-drenched interior. There was a man with several bullet holes in him in the driver's seat, dead as a doornail.

One of the cops, a large Irishman, was screaming into his radio for backup. Another wave of officers joined in the fray and started pushing the bystanders back away from the crime scene. Willie and I seized the moment and went to the vacant space the cops had created to videotape the crime scene. The victim was seated upright behind the wheel, with his eyes wide open.

"What happened?" Willie asked.

"This guy came out of a pawnshop," the cop explained, "got into this beat-to-shit Chevy Nova. Another car pulled next to him and shot him with a Mac ten."

There were a dozen bullet holes in the door and at least that many in him.

The big Irishman calling the shots was a sergeant. He was sweating like a stuck pig, and really getting pissed off. As the crowd started shoving again, I realized these assholes could crush us, and for what? Just for a glimpse at a dead guy? A few more cops got involved and shoved the angry horde back again.

Now, in those days the coroner had to show up to pronounce the victim officially dead before they could remove the body. Our Irish buddy knew this and was doing his best to keep these stupid assholes away till the coroner showed, but this situation was getting out of hand. If it went on much longer some of his men were going to get hurt. (Not to mention Willie and me who were firmly entrenched next to him like a couple of trapped rats.) It was total chaos, people were screaming, and then the shoving began again.

I was taping the scene, and Willie was holding the audio boom pole like a ball bat ready to take someone's head off if they got any closer. The people started to press forward again, and I could hear the sergeant yelling again, but this time he was yelling at me,

"Shut it off," he screamed. "Shut off the camera!"

I didn't understand at first, so he yelled it again.

"Shut off the camera! Put it down!"

I took the camera off my shoulder and set it down. As soon as I did, the sergeant flung open the car door, and in one single motion grabbed the dead body and slammed it to the ground. The pushing people stopped in their tracks. Women screamed, little children cried, and everyone froze right where they were. The Irishman screamed at them.

"Get your children out of here! Go home! Have some fucking decency!"

Slowly, the crowd backed up, and started to disperse. The sergeant looked at me and smiled. He picked the dead guy off the ground and stuffed his body back into the front seat of the car.

Two minutes earlier it was mayhem. Now it was damn near silent.

They just don't pay these guys enough.

\* \* \* \* \*

Soon after that experience we were back on Rush Street on another nice summer day. This time instead of sitting in the car looking at women, we pulled an old cameraman trick. We set the camera out on a tripod and acted like we were working. We had a fairly good batting average when we did this. God willing, women would appear and ask us about the news story of the day.

On this day, two of them appeared almost instantly.

"So," one of them asked, "Are you here for the murder that happened at the transient hotel across the street last night?"

We hadn't heard, but when we looked across the street we

saw a couple of undercover cops come out of the hotel. They spotted us too. One of the officers came across the street.

"Stay right where you are," he said with a little attitude in his voice. "This is still an active crime scene."

He seemed a little relieved when we told him our presence was just a coincidence and became a little more outgoing.

"So what's going on over there?" Willie asked.

"A prostitute brought a john back to the hotel with her," the cop explained. "She had sex with him, but instead of paying her, he slashed her to death. She got it real bad. There was blood everywhere. From what I could tell, she was a pretty girl."

"Do you have a positive ID on the body?" Willie asked.

"Yes, but I can't give you the name," the cop said.

"Was she blonde?" Willie pressed further. "Was she from down south?"

The officer perked up right away. "And you would know this how?" he asked.

We explained how we met her and how we always saw her with different guys. We even explained her nickname "Nasty." The officer took down a couple of notes, closed his notebook, smiled at us, and sighed.

"Well fellas, that's how your friend went out. Nasty."

# Chapter

# A MAN OF THE NIGHT

In every occupation, in every company, there always has to be at least one character. You know the kind of person I'm talking about. One person that people always tell stories about. NBC was no different. Our character was Pat Horton.

Pat was admired and feared throughout the business. He was bestowed with the nickname "The Vampire" because he only worked only the night shift and dressed totally in black, year round. He wore black boots, black pants, a black T-shirt, a black leather jacket, and a skull ring. He accented the look with slicked back hair and slightly greying teeth. Pat was a weight lifter, was into karate, and had a couple of tattoos, but he was also the most soft-spoken man I ever knew.

Pat never really had a steady partner because most guys got tired of his constant moving around. From the second he got on the clock, he'd load his gear in the live truck and would leave the building, heading nowhere special. He always drove, putting hundreds of miles on the truck every night. He'd just drive until he got the call for an assignment, and when he was done with the assignment, he went back to driving around the city.

The tales of Pat were legendary. He was known to frequent strip clubs in the NBC live truck; you know, the one with the peacock logo painted on the side. He parked it by the front door. Pat also brought cheeseburgers to give to the homeless and gave old books to prostitutes just because he liked talking to them.

Pat was the kind of guy who never started a fight, because he believed there was always a better solution. But when there was no other solution, he also never walked away from trouble, including one of the rare occasions I worked with him on a rainy evening on the city's far west side.

A couple of people had been killed that night. We finished our live shot, and we were wrapping up our equipment. When suddenly, out of nowhere, the neighborhood welcoming committee appeared. They were three local youth sporting the latest in NBA wear and displaying more gold than Tiffany's. They proudly showed us a couple of knifes and a zip gun.

"Hello Whitey," one of them said.

"Hello Honky," another one added.

They weren't smiling while addressing us. I figured these punks were young, and more bark than bite, but as I put our gear away I became increasingly leery of them. They were eyeing the contents of the truck, talking shit, and acting like big men.

Without any fanfare, a looming figure appeared from the shadows. It was the Vampire, and he was holding a long slim leather pouch. Pat stared them down and slowly pulled a pair of nun-chucks from the pouch. He stood there motionless.

The three looked at him and started laughing. The biggest one, sporting a fashionable retro Baltimore Bullets Wes Unseld jersey, stared at Pat from head to toe.

"Faggot," he said to Pat.

Pat's eyes narrowed. He flashed his gray teeth, and a look of disdain shot across his face. It was like a scene from "Enter The Dragon," only this time the role of Bruce Lee was played by an aging biker dressed totally in black. Pat's muscular, tat-covered arms, slicked back hair and skull ring on his middle finger went into action wheeling the nun-chucks across his body in a fury only the great Bruce Lee could match.

Under one arm, then over the shoulder, then across the body, over and over again, the nun-chucks were moving at a lightning-speed. He grunted as he shifted into high gear. The more he came at them, the more they backed off. He knew these were only misguided youth, so Pat was only in display mode, not kill mode, but it was still impressive.

The troublemakers appeared mesmerized by Pat's awesome exhibition. The Vampire pressed forward, whirling leg kicks, and twirling the sticks of pain. The punks were rightfully backing off, when all of a sudden, Pat twirled the sticks over his shoulder and smacked himself right in the nuts with a thud so loud and forceful it made my teeth rattle.

The punks fell silent.

They were in total shock.

But the Vampire never broke stride. If anything, the swinging of the nun-chucks seemed to intensify, and Pat appeared more determined than ever to drive away the potential evil forces before us. The three thugs took the hint, and walked away in disbelief. Pat didn't stop right away. He kept on going. His beady eyes were crossed, and he looked extremely pale.

"Are they gone?" he eked out.

"Yes, Pat, they walked away right in front of you," I replied.

But he barely heard me. He was now ashen. He grabbed one of the truck's door handles, steadied himself, and started to dry heave. He gingerly opened the truck door and threw his shattered body behind the wheel.

His balls may have been swollen to the size of grapefruits, but Pat still insisted on driving.

\* \* \* \* \*

That wasn't even the Vampire's most legendary clash. Scaring off neighborhood punks was nothing compared to scaring off the "Man." That story has been told countless years to all in Chicago's television circle who would listen. It's known simply as "The Broken Lunch."

Because we were a union shop, we had a firm list of rules and regulations that had to be followed. One of the rules was that we could have fifteen minutes to travel to lunch, and then we'd get a full hour for the lunch itself. In a city the size of Chicago, this was considered incredibly reasonable, and was never questioned until Assistant News Director Paula Eastman thought she could earn brownie points with the company. One day she instructed the assignment desk to eliminate all travel time for lunches. She said that from then on when the desk told us we were on lunch, no matter where we were, our lunchtime was to begin at that exact second.

The morning crews were the first ones peddled this crap, and the word spread like wildfire. The union stewards called the union to complain but found out there was no official language in the contract about travel time. It was only an unwritten rule. It seemed there was nothing they could do about it.

As legend has it, when the nighttime guys checked in for their shifts, there was a little impromptu meeting about how to handle this situation. Pat was asked to help, and he took a pass. That angered some of the guys, but Pat was calm.

"When the time comes," he said, "I will handle it."

As the evening wore on and the sun started to dip down on the horizon of Lake Michigan, Pat was stuck in traffic. Lake Shore Drive was bumper-to-bumper gridlock. A call came over the radio from the assignment editor.

"Sorry guys," she said. "Paula wants you on lunch this very minute."

"No problem," Pat said. "Put us on lunch right now, thanks."

He slammed the brakes on the truck, and came to a complete halt in the right lane of Lake Shore Drive.

"Grab your personal shit," Pat said to his partner. "We're leaving the truck."

And that's what they did. The two men exited the truck, locked it, and left it in the middle of rush hour traffic. They headed toward a park with picnic tables and a beautiful view of Lake Michigan, about five hundred feet from the impromptu gridlock that they left behind.

By this time Lake Shore Drive was up for grabs. People were honking their car horns, screaming at Pat and his partner Mike, making obscene gestures and a few unkind comments about their mothers. You have to remember, this was before cell phones, so no one could contact the police as quickly as they would have liked, but as fate would have it, one showed up pretty quickly. He was just as angry as the rest of the Chicagoans trapped in traffic. He pulled his car over a curb and onto the grass of the finely manicured park.

The officer started shouting before he even got out of his

squad car.

"You two assholes belong to that truck?"

Pat got off the park bench and addressed the officer. "Yes sir," he said. "That's our work vehicle."

The officer was now red faced and struggling to contain his emotions. "Then why the fuck aren't you working in it?"

"Because we are proving a point to the people back at the station who have never been on the street and don't know what we go through," Pat calmly explained.

"What the hell are you talking about?" the officer asked.

"Well, sir," Pat said, now searching for the words, "We work for people who are always looking for ways to cut corners with us. They don't appreciate the daily work we do for them. It's just take and never give."

"What the hell are you talking about?" the officer repeated.

"Sir, they took away our travel time for lunch," Pat explained.

The officer was taken aback.

"Wait a minute," he said. "You mean when they tell you to go to lunch, you're on lunch immediately, and no courtesy time?"

Pat nodded.

"That's bullshit," the officer said. "Even our people haven't tried that one." The officer smiled and nodded to Pat. "You got balls. This should get their attention." He raised his radio to his mouth and called his dispatcher, "Get me the NBC newsroom." He looked at Pat. "Who should I ask for?"

"Paula, ask for Paula," Pat replied.

Paula answered.

"Listen, you hear these horns honking in the background?"

he said to her.

"Yes," she replied.

"This is all thanks to your goddamn live truck. These guys are stopped here because you put them on lunch immediately. They just left their truck on Lake Shore Drive. It's becoming a very hostile situation here. If you don't order your employees to go back to work, we're going to impound the truck and fine NBC."

That got Paula's attention, and she reluctantly gave in.

"Your lunches are broken," she told Pat and his partner. "Come back to the station!"

Pat broke into a big grin.

'What does that mean?" the officer asked Pat.

"It means they have to pay us extra money for screwing with us," Pat said. He extended his hand to the officer. "Buy you a drink?"

"Shit," the officer replied with a smile. "You're buying all the drinks."

Back at the station Pat and Mike were hailed as heroes among the working folk. That move was never tried again, and even Paula's management co-workers lost respect for her.

Of course, it wasn't because of the dumb move she made.

It was because she had lost to one of us.

# Chapter

# THE TIMES ARE A-CHANGING

In 1986, General Electric bought NBC from RCA. Initially GE said they would change nothing about the operation and the way it was being run. We all knew that was bullshit. General Electric only cared about one thing—the bottom line.

First, they started getting rid of the old school guys in the newsroom. They were offered buyouts and other incentives to leave the job early. What the company didn't understand was that these were the guys who ran the news desk and made the daily news decisions. They had millions of contacts, knew the city like the back of their hands, and were a wealth of knowledge. In an instant the lifeblood of the newsroom had been replaced by young kids. These guys came from small markets at half the price.

If you walked by the conference room where the morning meeting was being held on any given day, you could see an accountant sitting shoulder to shoulder with an editorial person deciding what stories to cover based on expense or if overtime would be involved. Technology also started to rear its ugly head. A new brand of television camera combined audio and video into one. It would eventually be the end of the soundman and the two-man crew.

Of course, the station wanted the same amount of work

done by one guy that they used to get from two.

This was obviously a huge change for us. Being alone on the street was hard enough, but traveling alone was a whole other thing, especially going out of town. When you traveled with two guys, one guy was dropped off at the airport terminal with as much as eight cases of gear. His job was to take care of the tickets and tipping the skycaps so we didn't get charged extra for excess baggage, while the other guy parked the car in the airport garage. Doing both of those jobs was going to be a nightmare.

When it was time to select one of us to be the first one on the road by himself, the bean counters proved why they should have been stocking shelves in a toy store instead of making decisions about personnel.

They picked Willie.

The way he handled this situation only added to Willie's legend.

His destination was Kansas City, Missouri. He was supposed to meet our consumer reporter there. Willie pulled the crew car to the curb at the departure gate, popped the trunk, and watched as the skycap unloaded the gear and stacked everything on the curb.

"I'll be back," he said, just leaving thousands of dollars of gear unattended.

Twenty minutes later, he got off the shuttle parking bus and was dismayed to find the gear on the curb safe and sound.

Unsuccessful with Plan A (hoping someone would liberate the equipment), he moved on to Plan B. Willie handed the skycap his ticket.

"Sorry," he said, "it looks like I've got too much baggage

here. It looks like you're going to have to charge me extra."
Next he handed the skycap a ten-dollar bill for every piece of
equipment he was going to tag. "I believe this one is going to
Los Angeles, this one is going to Cleveland, and this one is going to Memphis."

Eighty dollars of tips got the bags to go to eight different
cities, none of which was Kansas City.

Willie landed in Missouri with nothing but the camera in
his hands. The consumer reporter met him by the baggage area
and saw he had the camera with one tape in it, but he had no
lights, no tripod, and no microphones. When she realized Willie had no support gear, she lost her mind.

"We can't do a shoot with no equipment!" she raged.

Willie had come through again. His balls and ingenuity
actually delayed the inevitable. Two man crews remained the
norm for out-of-town travel for quite a while after that debacle.
One case of gear was never found. We can only hope it wound
up somewhere warm.

\* \* \* \* \*

After General Electric took over all the NBC owned and
operated stations, the mood and style of the news, which had
been informative and in depth, was streamlined into a much
faster paced newscast.

The anchorman who once brought huge viewership was
now feeling the heat because the numbers for the news were
not so great anymore. It wasn't because he had lost his touch.
Viewership was down because the viewer had so many other
choices. Cable was exploding on the scene. CNN came out

of nowhere and intrigued everyone in the business with the way they covered the news from all over the world. The local news business was starting to shrink and the air talent were the first to feel the pinch. Younger, cheaper reporters and anchors replaced the veterans and their big salaries. Every remaining veteran was sweating it.

One hot summer Sunday afternoon that pressure bubbled over. In Gary, Indiana, a group of six African-American teenagers scaled a fence to a local city owned pool and went for a swim before it opened. What seemed to be just a little childhood mischief turned out to be tragic, because not one of these kids could swim. Three kids wandered into the deep end of the pool and never came out.

By the time our station got wind of the story, it was midafternoon. The first phone call went to Sam Raymond, my Cub trip buddy. Sunday was Sam's day off, but he knew better than to say no under the new General Electric reality. Paranoia was running rampant through all the reporters, and Sam was no exception.

Unfortunately, he had been drinking that day, and when he got the call he was feeling no pain. He agreed to do a live shot on the 5:00 News, even though he was not in any condition to do so.

I just happened to turn the television on the exact moment the anchorman tossed it to Sam. He was standing right by the pool where the tragedy occurred. I could tell immediately. I had seen that look on his face before. But that normally around 2am with the glow of a neon beer light illuminating his blood shot eyes. This was during the 5:00 News.

When he opened his mouth to speak, he started to slur his

words.

Why no one picked up on it before he went live was beyond me. Someone should have stopped him. It was so obvious that he was drunk. They shut off his microphone back at the station and went to video. All the viewers saw was a silent thirty second video of a swimming pool because Sam was supposed to talk over the live shot.

The video ended, and the anchorman came on the air.

"It looks like we're having some technical difficulties," he said.

I knew at that moment what was going to happen to Sam. If the station had ever thought of getting rid of Sam, they no longer had to look very far for a reason. He was screwed. He had tried to do the right thing and it backfired on him.

Three weeks later, they bought him out of the remaining portion of his contract and gave him a few months of salary. Sam took it like a man. He uprooted his family, said goodbye to his friends, and left town.

* * * * *

One would think that an incident like that would have made us think twice about drinking on the job, but only a month later Willie and I were working the Friday night shift and were sitting in a bar.

Willie's partner had gotten sick in the late afternoon and went home. I was finishing up my day shift, and the desk asked if I'd stay.

"It's a slow night," the woman at the desk said. "Just hop in the truck with Willie. He doesn't even have an assignment.

We'll only use you as a backup. We need someone just in case a plane crashes."

They didn't mean that literally, of course, that's just news speak for "in case the shit hits the fan." By nine o'clock, no shit had hit the fan, so we decided we needed a drink. We were on our second beer when the pager went off. Three convicts had escaped from a jail on 26th street.

"We need you live for the ten," the panicking woman on the assignment desk screamed on the phone.

"We'll make it!" Willie screamed back.

We were on the other side of town, but traffic was light. My lead foot got us there in less than twenty minutes. There were armed officers with dogs everywhere. Squad cars were racing up and down the tree-lined boulevard by the jail. Low flying choppers with searchlights were bathing the area with light, trying to get a glimpse of the fugitives.

The cops directed us to the media area where the other stations had their trucks parked already. As we pulled to our spot, we could see five-eight blonde reporter, Tina Sholman in her crotch-high skirt and spike-heeled shoes bathed in the copter lights.

Willie loved to mess with her because she was totally clueless when it came to sexual harassment, and Willie had a master's degree in it. As we piled out of the truck, Willie bee-lined toward her, only to be intercepted by the courier Frank Fontano. NBC hired off-duty Chicago police officers as couriers and bodyguards and Frank was one of their more aggressive hires. Couriers ran deliveries across town, drove reporters to meet crews, and when we wound up in shitty neighborhoods, they were given a pay upgrade to carry their guns and protect us.

Frank stood there with a real pissed off look on his face. His jacket was pulled back just enough to see the butt of his gun.

"Go easy, you black piece of shit" Frank barked at Willie.

"Fuck you! You wop," Willie barked back.

The two stood toe to toe for a moment, attracting the attention of everyone in the area, including local law enforcement. Frank was a born and raised on the streets kind of guy with a jet black pompadour, jeans and sweatshirts, and a fuck-you attitude. When things got hairy, Frank never hesitated to kick ass, and his work record showed it. He had tons of excessive force complaints against him, although nothing ever stuck.

The toe-to-toe confrontation was starting to make everyone a little nervous, when suddenly big smiles appeared on both Frank's and Willie's face, and they shook hands.

Frank hated blacks, but he loved Willie.

In record time, Willie and I threw up a live shot. The studio was screaming at us to get Tina in front of the camera, so she snapped to attention and was ready to go. As the studio gave her a fifteen-second cue, a chopper hit us with a spotlight essentially backlighting Tina. Her white blouse and dress were now virtually see-through.

"Holy shit!" Frank said when he saw her.

With all the noise and activity going on all around her, Tina held her composure until Willie got on an internal microphone we call the interrupt, where he could talk to Tina in her earpiece.

"You have lovely breasts," he whispered, "and we can all see them."

Her eyes began darting to see who noticed her nearly naked

state, and she started to ramble.

"Um, the police are looking for three black men in orange jump suits, and, um, as you might imagine that might be hard to find in this all-black neighborhood, where um, that kind of attire is often seen on the streets."

That brought on a roar of laughter from Frank, Willie, and I.

As soon as she was off camera, Tina threw the microphone to the ground.

"You fucker! You prick!" she screamed at Willie. "I hate you!"

Tina stormed toward the courier car, opened the door, then slammed it so hard it was a wonder that the window didn't explode. Willie fell to the ground in a state of sheer belly laughter. Frank came over and helped him up. Both men had tears in their eyes and were having trouble breathing because of the constant laughing.

A group of state police came over to the two men.

"Hey assholes, keep it down," one of them said. "We're conducting an active manhunt here."

Frank went from a smile to a sneer in an instant. He pulled out his badge.

"Fuck you, trooper pussies. You're in my jurisdiction now. You're not real cops, and I don't take orders from you. Take those sissy hats you wear and go write tickets on the expressways where you belong!"

The troopers gave us dirty looks and walked away meekly. Frank shook his head, walked back to the car, and got Tina out of there. She gave us the finger as she drove by.

It was at that point it dawned on the two of us that we were still semi-drunk, and we had a bit of a problem.

"Where can we piss around here?" I asked Willie. The search activity was starting to move farther down the street toward the south and Willie had a bright idea.

"Why don't we make our way into the middle of the boulevard and piss by the bushes?" he suggested.

"In the middle of the street?" I asked.

"Yeah, why not? In the darkness we'll just look like two more cops conducting a search."

This sounded totally absurd to me, but I was about to burst. So, like a mindless dumbass, I followed. We weaved our way between, through, and around what seemed like every cop in a five state area until we made it to the bushes. Willie was right. Not a soul noticed, and not a moment too soon. I had to go so bad that the second my zipper went down it sounded like I was dousing the bushes with a fire-hose. My piss was so forceful there was a good chance I was going to uproot the very bushes we were using for cover.

"Oh shit," Willie whispered over his own fire-hose sound effects. "Listen."

With that, a chopper roared in from nowhere, and before I could reel in my little buddy, we were under the chopper's spotlight— now the center of attention of the entire search party. Barking dogs approached us, closely followed by a pack of police officers.

"Freeze!" one of them yelled as I discreetly attempted to tuck my friend back into my pants. It was the same trooper that Frank had screwed with a few minutes earlier.

We were lucky they didn't take it out on us too badly. After excessive questioning, we were told to get out of the area.

But our Friday night was only beginning. Our desk told

us to head to a nearby police station, because the fugitives would be taken there if they were apprehended. Most of the other stations in town were there, and all of them had the same look on their faces— that unmistakable "we're going to be here all night" look. We just knew we had all blown our Friday night.

That feeling of dread changed instantly when a live truck from the local CBS station drove up. The sliding door opened, and the cameraman popped out holding a beer. The reporter and truck operator followed behind. They were all loaded, but they were there to share the wealth. All the camera guys in the city got along really well, and our friends from CBS had a case of beer on ice in the back of the live truck. Now we were all on overtime, drinking beer, and catching up with some old friends.

In the distance, the sirens were closing in fast. Officers from inside the station came running outside and took positions in the street right in front of us. We dropped the beers and grabbed our cameras. A squad pulled up to the front of the police station, and all the cameramen made a mad dash toward the back door of the squad car as it opened.

One of the three desperados, still wearing the orange jail-issued jumpsuit, emerged smiling from ear to ear.

"It's nice to see all of you," he said.

When a reporter shouted to him if he had any advice to the other two fugitives still on the run, he paused and muttered, in a low tone:

"Be down."

The officers walked him into the building, and we all looked at each other. I was very uneducated in my street slang, so I had to defer to the grand wizard of street wit and wisdom, Willie.

"What does 'Be down' mean?" I asked.

"Fuck if I know," he said.

# Chapter

## GOODBYE FRANK, HELLO SMALL TOWNS

I loved that NBC hired off duty cops as couriers because they hired some real characters. It was fascinating to sit in our crew room and listen to the stories they told about their days on the job. The older guys would talk about the days when they would get bribes from motorists to get out of traffic tickets, before they invented internal investigations. The real old guys had even more shocking stories.

"There used to be a high-priced whorehouse on Lake Shore Drive," one of them told me, "and we would wait until the women were on their way home. Then we'd pull them over for, say, a broken taillight, which had been mysteriously broken shortly after we pulled them over. You'd be amazed what girls like that would do to get out of a ticket."

Another old cop told us one prostitute got so tired of replacing taillights every night, she cut a deal to bypass the pulling over process and simply waited for certain officers in the parking lot of the whorehouse and took care of business there.

One night I was on live truck duty with Eddie Brooks, a guy who had worked the night shift for years. We were loitering at the news desk, just killing time. The desk person heard a shooting come across the scanner on the far South Side and asked us to head that way.

"Virginia will go with you," she said, of the station's lone female bodyguard. "She'll meet you by the elevators."

As we walked to the elevator, Eddie had a strange look on his face.

"Ever work with Virginia before?" he asked.

"Why would you ask me that?"

"Because man, when she's here in the building, she's a quiet loner, but when she's out on the streets, she turns into something completely different. She gets really keyed up."

"Keyed up? Like how?"

"I mean like cussing and really talking loud," Eddie answered back.

"Bullshit," I said. I couldn't picture it. There was no way.

When we got to the elevator, she was there, her quiet, smiling self. We exchanged pleasantries, the elevator door opened, we stepped in, and as the doors were about to close, an arm shot through, opening the doors again.

"I'm sorry, guys," the news director Dick said. "Don't mean to hold you up."

The elevator started our 19-floor descent, and Virginia reached to her ankle and pulled out a small handgun. No one said a word. We just watched as she opened it, and checked to see if it was loaded. She put that one back, reached under her jacket and pulled out a much bigger gun. She opened it and took the magazine out.

"You guys going to a bad neighborhood?" Dick asked, laughing.

Before Eddie or I could answer, Virginia snapped at him with some serious attitude.

"What the fuck constitutes a bad neighborhood?" she

asked. "Where black people live? If that's what you mean, then why don't you drag your white ass along with us, and you'll get to see some dead niggers."

The elevator bell dinged, the door opened, and Virginia stormed out.

Eddie held the door open, and Dick walked past us. He didn't look either Eddie or me in the eye, but I can still picture the expression on his face.

He looked like he had just wet himself.

\* \* \* \* \*

Of all the characters, my favorite by far was Frank Fontano. I'm sure his first word as a child was either a racial slur or street slang for a female body part. This guy could make a sailor blush. He always wore a sweatshirt and blue jeans with black gym shoes and a Members Only jacket, and he always had an unlit cigarette hanging from the left side of his mouth.

Frank was married to his high school sweetheart, and when he spoke of his wife and their three kids, he seemed like a normal, loving, caring individual who only wanted the best for his family. On the other hand, our friend also had some pretty obvious anger issues, and his face showed the signs of it. Frank had a couple of teeth missing on the side of his mouth, and every time he smiled, that was the first thing you noticed. The good news is that when you saw Frank smiling, at least you knew he was happy and safe to approach.

One day, he was overcome with joy. The police board didn't have enough evidence to fire him after it was alleged he caught a teenage boy stealing from a supermarket, and threw the kid through a plate glass window. Frank told me he and his partner saw the kid running from the store, and caught him a couple of blocks later.

"I put this kid's hands behind his back," he said, "And the kid called me a pig. I politely told him that wasn't called for because I'm an officer of the law and that demanded his respect. So what does this kid do? He calls me, Officer Pig."

Not good.

"So I looked right and left for witnesses, and then launched the kid through a department store window. The kid's parents filed charges, but three witnesses magically appeared with tales of how I fought off the much younger and stronger criminal," Frank said with a twinkle in his eye.

"During the struggle, your honor, the kid must have somehow fallen through the window."

Frank loved that one. He couldn't keep a straight face telling that story.

My favorite Frank story is when reporter, Lori Norman, and I enlisted Frank's services to protect us while we were doing a story in the Cabrini Green housing project. At the time, this low-income facility was the most dangerous location in Chicago.

Frank figured if we arrived around 10am, it would be a piece of cake, nice and safe.

The story was about a fifteen-year-old girl who had concealed her pregnancy from her mother for the entire length of her term. (Not an easy thing to do with four people living in a one-bedroom apartment.) The secret to her success had been wearing oversized clothes.

We settled into the bedroom with the girl and her newborn, and the camera was rolling when shots suddenly erupted throughout the housing project corridors so loudly the baby jumped, almost causing the girl to drop her child.

Frank entered the room moments later. He ordered us all into the tiny hallway just adjacent to the living room, and put the five of us (Lori, the girl with the baby, the girl's mother, and me) against the wall. The shots were reverberating through the stairwells, and the residents were screaming. It was a hectic scene. The curtains were drawn in our little hideaway, but we could see a constant stream of silhouettes, people running back and forth in front of the window.

I glanced at Frank. He had his gun drawn and was prepared for whatever was going to come through that door. In the midst of all confusion, that goofy bastard grinned at me.

"I got six shots," he whispered. "After that, you fucks are on your own."

The mother of the girl must have picked up on the fact that Frank was going to waste whoever walked through her front door, so she stood up and charged my Italian friend.

"Mister, mister, don't shoot," she pleaded. "My boy is out there, and he's coming home, Sonny's out there!"

She grabbed Frank's right arm, the one that was holding the gun, but Frank's left hand grabbed her right wrist and twisted her to the ground.

"Get your fucking hands off me," he barked. "I'll shoot your ass and wait the rest of the day just to blow fucking Sonny away too! Understand, lady? Anyone that comes through that door dies!"

As soon as those words left Frank's lips, a door behind us opened, and a voice from a darkened room asked what was going on. Frank spun around and pointed the gun at the head of a 16-year-old boy.

"Are you Sonny?" Frank asked

"No man, I'm James," the kid said. "I was sleeping, man."

Sure as shit, this kid opened the door of the room he was in and flipped on the light. It was the bathroom, and inside the bathtub, there was a small mattress. The bathroom was doubling as James' bedroom.

While I was surveying the bath/bedroom I felt Lori grab my arm and let out a heavy gasp. I'd never seen her eyes get so wide. Lori was focused on James' crotch. He was wearing only underwear, and it barely concealed his foot long hard-on. James smiled at Lori, which caused her to grasp my arm even tighter.

"Get your black ass back in that room and get decent," the boy's mother screamed, and James retreated.

All the blood was drained from Lori's face. She was more shaken by her brief encounter with a well-hung bathroom dweller than she had been by the gunplay, which had finally dissipated.

"Let's get the fuck out of here," Frank said.

He slowly opened the front door, and it appeared the coast was clear. Frank was in the lead with his gun drawn, and Lori and I followed behind him. We went down four flights of stairs, looking in every direction and studying every face. Once we hit ground level, Frank covered us as I stowed away the gear. It was incredibly tense.

Lori and I both finally got seated, and Frank got us the hell out of there. Nobody said a word for a few moments. After we were finally free and clear, Frank cut the silence by looking at Lori in the rear view mirror.

"That was some crank on that shine, huh?" he said, flashing his toothless smile.

Frank died of heart failure about three years later.

Yes, he was crude, but he also was a product of the street, pure and true to his environment. To this day, I still think about Frank, and my memories of him still make me smile.

\* \* \* \* \*

I rarely traveled, but as time went on, I made friends with the guys in the network bureau, so when the network crew guys went on vacation, I got to fill in for them.

On July 2nd, 1986, cameraman Johnny C. asked me to travel to a small town in Nebraska for a Fourth of July live shot wrap-around of a parade in a small town to be broadcast on NBC's Today Show. The idea was to do a series of live shots from progressively bigger towns, winding up eventually with the big parade in New York City. Our destination was a small town located about sixty miles from Omaha, Nebraska.

There were four of us on this assignment: Johnny, a producer named Stan, the correspondent, James, and me. We arrived in town midday on July 3rd. As we pulled our rented Lincoln Town Car through the main street of town, every head turned. People stopped in their tracks and blatantly stared.

"This is like those sci-fi movies where the aliens land on earth and all the town folk are just stunned to see them," Johnny said.

Without missing a beat, James was a little more realistic.

"These country boys have never seen a black man before," he said.

James wasn't just black; he was dark black. After a warm welcome and a thirty-second tour of the whole town, we were treated to lunch. We met various members of the city council; Billy Bob, Carl, Norman, and seventy-five-year old Tommy Joe, the Mayor.

At this lunch meeting, I saw the evil genius of Johnny C. in action. These people had never had any nationwide recognition before, and Johnny was going to have some fun with them. He excused himself from the table, and strolled out into the main street. Johnny was acting like he was looking through a camera lens, kneeling down on the street, looking at all angles, and putting on quite a show for the small town folks.

"Johnny is a visionary," Stan pointed out to the table of dignitaries. "He's mentally framing out the entire parade in his head."

The locals were eating it up, and I was struggling not to burst into laughter. We moved outside and onto Main Street. Once everyone gathered around the Francis Ford Coppola imitator, he smiled and directed his full attention right at the mayor.

"I'd like to do a run through, a dry run, a warm up," Johnny said. "I want to see what will happen tomorrow."

The mayor seemed very taken aback by Johnny's request, but you could tell he wasn't going to refuse the great one. The mayor nodded his okay to Johnny and threw his minions into action. In less than two hours, approximately 400 people were assembled in the downtown area. The high school band that was to lead off the parade was there in full force, no easy task considering that they were on summer vacation. The floats, the cars decorated for the town dignitaries, and the fire and police cars were also assembled at the behest of one man.

Johnny and I broke out the camera gear and assembled it on the street corner that provided the best vantage point to capture the entire parade. The town folk were eating out of Johnny's hand, and he was taking full advantage of it. He walked over and stood in front of a liquor store.

"A cold beer sure would taste great while I'm figuring out the logistics of this live shot," he announced.

Before you knew it, we were drinking ice-cold beer on Main Street.

After a few more minutes of busy work and acting for the locals, Johnny shouted to the eager crowd.

"Take your places, everyone. It's time to do a dry run."

On cue, the entire town fell in line. The band played, everyone marched by, Johnny panned the camera to the people who lined the streets, and everyone waved and cheered. The whole thing took five minutes. When everything calmed down Johnny turned to me.

"These poor bastards don't know the live shot is only forty-five seconds long," he whispered.

Although everything seemed to work out just fine, Johnny wasn't done. He eyed a flatbed truck parked in an alley and persuaded the owner to put us on the flatbed. He wanted him to elevate us, and when the parade started, slowly lower us to ground level. It was a poor man's dolly shot, but it worked.

Johnny also quickly realized there was a potential problem on the horizon. James' dark skin combined with the backlight from the early morning sun was going to make him look like a raisin, so Johnny placed a call to New York in search of a light strong enough to combat the sun and make our guy look good.

He was told a 5k Fresnel light would be hand delivered by a company out of Omaha by 6am the next morning, right before our shot. I didn't have a clue what a 5k Fresnel light was until Johnny explained it.

"It's the type of light they use for movies, the big round ones. So much heat will come off this thing he'll almost glow."

That night, the big-time television people were the guests of honor at a local diner with fried chicken and corn on the cob. The local residents gave speeches about how happy they were to have us there and how we were going to put their little town on the map.

When there was a lull in the activity, Johnny and I snuck out of the restaurant, leaving Stan and James to fend for themselves. We walked across the street to the liquor store, grabbed a twelve pack of beer, hopped in the Town Car, and took off.

Outside the city limits, Johnny decided to show me some maneuvers he learned in a stunt driving class he'd just taken. Our tires were screeching, and gravel was flying everywhere. We were a couple of goofs laughing it up on a warm Nebraska night. After various reenactments of stunt driving 101 we came to rest in a small park overlooking the skyline of our new favorite small town. We were at least three beers in when, out of nowhere, a local cop pulled up. He wandered over to us.

"Hello, boys," he said. "I saw a fifty foot dust cloud. That ain't the sort of thing we see out here too much. I thought I best investigate."

We were blatantly in violation of the law. For starters, we were drinking open alcohol in public, but as we stood with beers in hand, the officer thanked us for coming to his town and said he wanted to express his appreciation for everything we were doing.

"Listen fellas," he said, "Can I ask you a favor?"

"Sure," Johnny said.

"Tomorrow during the parade, can you focus your camera on my daughter? Can't miss her. She's the only redhead playing the flute in the marching band."

"You got it, sir," Johnny said.

He left after that assurance, but we didn't. We sat out there bullshitting until 2am, but we had to be on Main Street at 4:30 in the morning for a 7am east coast hit. Needless to say, we hadn't exactly been using our heads. I got about a half hour of sleep and took a hot shower, and somehow, miraculously, I really didn't feel that bad.

The sun hadn't come up yet, but Johnny felt compelled to walk around with his dark shades on, talking to everyone who would listen. At 6am on the dot, the light showed up. We mounted it on the flatbed, ran the power, set the camera, and we were ready to go. A satellite truck had showed up in the middle of the night, so we hooked up to that. New York had our picture in a matter of minutes.

The sun slowly rose and bathed the small town in an orange glow. James hopped in front of the camera. With the combination of the light we were throwing on him and the backlighting from the sun, the scene looked like a beautiful painting. The director in New York raved how great everything looked.

We had it all worked out. After we got the ten-second cue from New York, Stan was going to wave his hand, signaling the band to start playing. He then would cue the guy operating the flatbed, who from there would slowly lower us down. We would have James in the picture the entire time, with the parade and the town in the background, displayed in all of its glory. As soon we hit the ground, New York would throw it to another city, and we would be done.

There is nothing like a good plan going to shit on nationwide television. New York gave us the cue, Stan waved for the band to start, and for the first time since the rehearsal they were badly out of tune. The band sounded so bad James started to laugh when he introduced them. We cued the flatbed operator to lower us, but when he did, our smooth decent downward was anything but smooth. I grabbed James' leg so he didn't fall off the flatbed. We stopped and started, jerked up and then down, it was a thirty-second mess, even shorter than the forty-five seconds that had been planned.

When we hit the ground, the director spoke into our earphones.

"You're clear, Nebraska. That was interesting to say the least. Better luck next time."

Johnny stared a hole through the flatbed operator. The guy just gave us a weird look and walked away. The mayor who had been watching it on a television in a nearby hardware store came over to us.

"That wasn't quite what we were hoping for," he said, "but thanks for trying."

Stan, ever the politician, tried explaining the dangers of live television to the mayor. James just shook his head and laughed.

"All that for a thirty-second turd, let's get the hell out of here."

The next sixty miles were quiet until Stan spoke out.

"You ever wonder how a business can stay afloat operating the way this one does? Four round trip airplane tickets, four hotel rooms, a light rental, a flatbed rental, meal per diem and whatever else we could scam, all for a thirty-second live shot."

After another extended period of silence, Johnny put it all in perspective.

"This business is just a license to print money."

# Chapter

## THE FARMER AND HAROLD

The network gigs were not all feature shoots or updates on heart transplant patients. Sometimes they were hurry-up-and-go type stories. One day, I got a call to get to Midway Airport right away. A King Air plane was waiting for four of us: David, the field producer, Barbra, the correspondent, Susan, and me. We took off during a snowstorm in a small tin can with wings, certainly not one of my favorite things to do.

After we got above the clouds, I was finally able to pull my balls out of my throat and focus on Barbra's explanation of the story we were about to cover.

"We're heading to a town of about five hundred people: Hills, Iowa," she said over the noises of our herky-jerky tin can. "A sixty-three-year-old farmer there got up from bed this morning, had breakfast with his wife, shot her to death, then went next door and did the same thing to his neighbor. After that, he loaded up his truck and went into the local savings and loan and shot the bank's president. Five minutes later, he was stopped by local police on Main Street, and while the cops were waiting for backup, he stuck his twelve gauge shotgun in his mouth and ventilated the back of his skull."

When we arrived at Main Street, they were towing the blood-filled truck through the center of town. Downtown was about three blocks long and both sides of the street were bumper to bumper with satellite trucks.

Through the eerie, snow-swirling snowstorm and deafening wind, I took video of the bank, the president's office, the broken glass, and the blood. We talked to some of the locals on the streets, and they were just as stunned by the day's events as we were. Our journey eventually led us to the house where the whole thing started. The state police had roped the area off, but you couldn't help but marvel at the enormity of the land that this man owned. His home was dwarfed by acres and acres of farmland.

We went to a neighbor's house, a man in his late sixties, and asked about the man who had just gone on this rampage.

"He was my friend," the man said. "Salt of the earth. He was a hardworking and dedicated family man. The banker told him to use his farm's equity to buy more and expand, so he did. He bought more tractors and built bigger barns. When the economy went bad, the same banker that had told him to expand, told him 'Sorry, your note is due.' That farm has been in his family for a hundred years. He became inconsolable by the thought of losing the farm that his parents left him."

The man stopped talking, and took a breath to compose himself.

"Good people. Why he killed, I can't answer."

After we got everything we needed, we grabbed our gear, and headed back to the airfield. It was mid-afternoon, and we needed to get to the closest big city to feed the video and make the Nightly News cast. The pilots were waiting for us with extremely nervous looks on their faces.

"Des Moines is the closest feed point," one of them said.

"Problem is there's one hell of a storm brewing between here and there."

That kind of stopped us in our tracks. Barbra looked at the pilot.

"We've got to try," she said timidly.

He nodded, and off we went. We sat in four cramped seats, close together in back. The two pilots were behind a cabin door, which they kept closed on takeoff. The sound of the engines were so loud in the cabin we had to yell at each other to communicate. After we were airborne, the plane started gliding sideways. The more it climbed, the more it felt like it was sliding to the side. Suddenly the whole plane dropped in elevation, and not just a little, but fifteen to twenty feet. Once we leveled off, the door to the cockpit swung open and, with a very concerned look on his face, the co-pilot sternly commanded our attention.

"Stay buckled up," he said. "We are going headlong into a very big storm."

I saw the radar screen behind him, and it looked as if we were about to be swallowed up by a giant sea of white. No sooner had he turned back to the controls, when wham, we were engulfed in the storm. Hail started slamming hard on the planes exterior.

I looked out the window, and all I could see was the little light on the wing, spinning in the fury of the storm. David was to my right, and the girls were directly in front of me. We were bouncing so hard that I kept wondering how the plane was even holding together. We were all speechless. Barbra had tears in her eyes and a death grip on the seat's armrest. Susan had an unlit cigarette in her mouth. All the blood had drained from her face.

David, on the other hand, was the total opposite. I looked to my right, and he had his eyes closed like he was thinking of taking a nap. I elbowed him.

"How the hell can you be so calm?"

"What do you want me to do?" he asked. "Start screaming? Not a goddamn thing we can do."

The copilot turned around.

"There's a cooler behind you," he said in a wavering voice. "Might as well drink something."

He slammed the cockpit door closed behind him.

The word "drink" caught my attention, and I swung my arm around behind the seat to grab the cooler. It had a bottle of wine and six beers. The girls grabbed the wine like it was a winning lottery ticket. I offered a beer to David, who declined. He had given up drinking years earlier. I was kind of glad he declined the offer because I knew I might need all six of those beers. I wanted to numb my body before we nosedived head first into a cornfield.

The girls were holding hands and hugging. (Even in the midst of this death ride, I was hoping for a little lesbian action, but to no avail.) We were dropping and then climbing and dropping again, when the plane finally started to gain altitude. All of a sudden, we broke through the storm, then through the clouds, and in the distance we even saw the sun.

The cockpit door sprung open, and the smiling co-pilot declared we were skipping Des Moines, staying above the clouds and heading back to Chicago. The three of us let out a collective sigh of relief. David snored. At this point, the farmer didn't matter, nor did small town Iowa, or even our employer, The Nightly News. When we touched down and exited the plane, the only reason I didn't drop to my knees and kiss the ground was because my bladder was full and I would have never gotten up off the tarmac.

Sure enough, I had consumed all six beers.

* * * * *

In November of 1987, Harold Washington had a heart attack in his fifth floor office in City Hall. At the time, I happened to be on the city's northwest side doing a story on the city's inability to control the growing rat problem in neighborhood alleys.

The reporter on the assignment with me, Tim Moreno, had just turned in his notice the day before. He hated the station's management and the way they ran things. Tim was from the East Coast and had landed a job in Washington. Tim was one of those guys that appeared to have a chip on his shoulder, but when you really got to know him you realized he was just cynical and had a dark sense of humor. We were in a rat filled alley when a call on the radio came from our news desk that the mayor had been rushed to a downtown hospital. Our assignment was to head back to the city and receive instructions from there. As we exited the Ohio Street exit and entered downtown, the desk called again.

"Ask the people on the street if they've heard about the mayor. If they have, ask how they feel about it. If they haven't heard, break the news to them and get their reaction on camera."

"Do we even know if he's dead or not?" Tim asked.

"No," the desk replied. "So ask two different versions. One

time say that he's still alive, and one time say that's he's dead."

This request sent Tim through the roof. He called them every name in the book. The great thing about our radio system was that every crew on the street heard every transmission. The heckling that ensued was relentless. Everyone thought it was a goofy idea, but we followed orders. We pulled over near a bus stop, I broke out the camera, and we sought out our interviewees.

The first interview was with a black woman. She burst into tears and ran away when Tim told her the news. The second one was a homeless guy with no teeth, and every other word he said was "asshole." The third was a well-dressed white man who looked like he was on his way to close a big business deal.

"What's your first reaction to the news that Mayor Washington had a heart attack?" Tim asked.

"Good," the man said.

Tim handed me the microphone and went home. I called the desk and was informed the mayor had passed. They stationed me at city hall to follow the rumors that a temporary successor to the mayor was going to be appointed. Sure enough, later that day an alderman was appointed temporary mayor. The appointee was a good guy, but the problem was he was white. That wasn't going to sit well with the ever-growing black population who had just lost their very first mayor. All this was happening while Harold Washington's body was being taken to a south side funeral home for the wake.

The next couple of days brought much speculation on who would succeed the mayor. The full city council met to choose the heir to the throne. The white aldermen chose a black alderman from the South Side of the city. The white aldermen knew it was suicide if they put one of their own in power, so they picked a guy they could seemingly control. After this incredibly long session ended, the city finally got around to the business of mourning their fallen leader.

The following day, a procession drove from the funeral home, through the area neighborhoods onto the expressway, and to city hall, where his body was scheduled to lie in state for two days. We were told the procession was going to be covered in pool-type fashion, meaning one television crew and one newspaper still photographer would ride along and serve all the other media outlets.

Peter and I were the guys chosen to have the privilege. We were to ride on the flatbed truck through the streets of Chicago in frigid temperatures. They told us to dress warm. I have felt very privileged to see some things that most people won't see, and this was one of those events I will never forget. Thousands of people lined the streets of Chicago's neighborhoods; everyone stood in cold temperatures and intermittent freezing rain. Kids saluted and grownups cried as the hearse passed slowly by. Paul was on camera and I on sound. Next to us was a still photographer from the Chicago Tribune.

The ride was a bit rocky because all we had to hold on to were the wooden side rails of the flat truck. For miles, we rode at one steady pace until we finally hit the expressway. Then we started to gain some speed.

The first two cars in the procession were Chicago police cars, followed by a limo with family members in it, the hearse, us in our flatbed, and a Chicago police car behind us. As soon as we approached downtown, suddenly the flatbed swerved to the right and then to the left before the driver got the truck under control and straightened us out.

Peter grabbed me for leverage and I grabbed the still photographer to stop him from falling out of the truck. A car had come out of nowhere and cut us off. The police car that was behind us raced ahead and pulled next to the Cadillac that had taken our spot in the procession. After thirty seconds of the officer talking to the strange car through open windows, it backed off and fell back in line.

The procession pulled to the west side of the city hall, and Peter and I hopped off the truck to get a shot of the casket coming out of the hearse and into the building. People slowly filed out of their cars, and we both waited patiently to see which asshole was getting out of the car that had cut us off. It was a black female alderman and her driver. She was one of the mayor's biggest supporters, a big mouth with plenty of attitude.

When they passed us, I couldn't help myself.

"You know that you cut us off, don't you?" I said.

They glared at me with a "fuck you" expression on their faces. Peter leaned to me.

"Let's get these assholes," he whispered.

I noticed a big Irish-looking cop sizing up the alderman's car. Seizing the moment, I approached the officer.

"It's really too bad," I said.

The cop looked at me in an inquisitive manner. "What do you mean?" he asked.

"Well officer," I said, "when they pulled their car here, I said 'you shouldn't park there, because the officers could give you a ticket.' Do you know what they said?"

"What?" he inquired.

"They said, 'Fuck the cops.'"

His eyes grew wide, and he grabbed his radio.

"We'll show them who's going to get fucked," he said.

Forty-five seconds later, the tow truck arrived, and the car was hooked and gone. I wish they could have seen their new Cadillac up on the tow truck hook.

\* \* \* \* \*

The next day I went to city hall and took video of the thousands of people that passed by Harold's casket. After about a half an hour, I started to smell this really weird burning odor. I couldn't put my finger on where it was coming from.

"You smell that?" a friend of mine from the ABC station leaned over and asked me.

"Yeah," I said. "What in the world is that?"

"The lights they're using to illuminate the casket are way too strong. He's baking like a two-day-old hot dog under the heat lamp at a Seven Eleven."

The following day church bells rang throughout all of Chicago. It was a day of mourning for a city that lost their leader. The hearse passed at least two thousand people waiting outside the church. It was packed wall-to-wall with politicians, friends, and enemies of the late mayor. They were all there to pay their respects and get their shot to stand at the pulpit and grandstand for the cameras.

After the service, about a mile or two from the cemetery, the people started chanting "Harold, Harold." It reminded me of a night when he was campaigning for his second term, shaking hands in Greek Town. He walked into every restaurant and bar on that five-block strip, eating at every stop. Every time he hit the sidewalk and went to the next establishment, crowds would chant for him with "Harold, Harold."

After the gravesite service, the crowds left, and it began to settle in that Harold was not coming back. The city was left to move forward without him.

The replacement mayor put in by the white majority of alderman was dropped like a hot potato when the next election came around. Richard M. Daley, the son of the late great Richard J. Daley, coasted to an easy victory, and for the next 22 years he reigned supreme.

# Chapter

## DEATH AND CHEATING DEATH

There were times when I came across things on the job that changed my view on life. I've always viewed this job as a giant window. Every day, I looked through it, and for better or worse, I was expected to document what appeared before me without opinion or emotion.

Some days that was almost impossible.

The day that hit me the hardest, the one that made me question society, was May 20, 1988. It was a Friday, I had planned to hook up with some buddies that evening and attend an old friend's bachelor party. I was looking forward to the strippers, beer, and cigars in store for me that night. My assignment was an easy one—I was to go Halas Hall, the training facility for the Chicago Bears in Lake Forest, Illinois and meet our new sports reporter, Tom Stanton. He was a fairly well-known radio reporter in town who had made the jump to television, and we were supposed to gather interviews with Bears players for a sports special that was going to air in the months to come. Before the team let us into the building, Tom and I had a chance to talk, and I found him to be a very pleasant guy.

"So," I said, "You like the news game?"

"I like the sports news game," he said. "I'm a sports fanatic, but I don't really know all that much about the hard news side of the business."

"You have no interest in it?" I asked.

"Zero," he admitted.

Shortly after those words left his mouth, my radio went off. It was our news desk. The assignment woman told me to get to Winnetka, a village about fifteen miles away, and she had urgency in her voice.

"There's been a shooting at a school," she said, "and it sounds like someone has been killed."

"I'm heading back to the station," Tom said when he heard that.

"Don't think so," I snapped, "You're going there with me. If it's as big as they say, I'll need your help."

Tom got in his car and followed me to Winnetka. On the drive there, I figured this was a false alarm and that the desk heard something wrong. I was certain that in no time we'd be turning around and heading back to Bears camp. That thought was quickly put to rest when I turned a corner and saw a school being descended upon by ambulances and squad cars.

I parked the car and grabbed my camera, pointing it at the side of the school. To my surprise, a door opened and a man, presumably a teacher, stepped out. He was staring blankly at me. When he stretched his arms upward, I could see his shirt was soaked in blood. He stood there amongst all the chaos that was starting to form around him.

No one noticed him but me.

I could feel my body tense up.

"Take a breath," I told myself. "Breathe, dammit, breathe."

The camera I was holding felt heavy on my shoulder, and my legs felt like they were about to give way. This was more than just taking video of someone.

The man slowly rubbed his hand across his shirt, and only then did he appear to realize the blood wasn't his. The man was blank with emotion, in shock and paralyzed with fear. A paramedic approached him, threw a blanket over his shoulders, and led him away.

Child after child was brought past the police tape flapping in the wind to their anxiety-ridden parents. The anguish and emotion these parents displayed as they waited to see if their child was alive or dead was difficult to watch. Crime scene detectives went in and out of the school, carrying evidence bags with bloody souvenirs left behind by a woman who had caused all this for no apparent reason.

As the day wore on, this became a national story. We sketched together what had happened. A woman by the name of Laurie Dann had walked into this elementary school sporting two handguns and opened fire on a second grade class. When the shooting ended, one person was dead, five others were wounded, and Laurie Dann had gotten away.

It's hard to describe the emptiness I felt, watching parents running alongside their children as the paramedics were pushing their gurneys toward the ambulance. That was bad enough, but there was one sight that brought the entire crime scene to a standstill.

The body bag containing the victim, an eight-year-old boy.

The faint sounds of crying were all but silenced by the whirling of the news choppers that filled the now overcast sky above the small village. As afternoon turned to night, it was time to go live with the story for our newscast and many of the NBC affiliates around the country. Since the woman was still on the loose, the town was on a lock down, which meant very little movement by anyone, no traffic in or out.

My new friend Tom was instantly turned into a news reporter. For a man thrown into one of the biggest stories that year, Tom stepped up to the plate and knocked it out of the park. Tom told the story with just the right amount of authority. My pictures accompanied his narration, and he made the viewers feel what we were feeling.

While Tom was into a live shot, word came from the director that police had trapped the woman in a house a few blocks away. Tom vamped long enough for a live picture to be taken from that scene to coincide with his live shot. He was rolling, live shot to live shot, and getting rave reviews from our management and managers from around the country.

The fun I had planned with my friends for that evening was now a distant thought. Tom kept doing his thing, now focusing on the woman held up in the house. We were using live pictures from the other crew as his scene setter. More information came in about her. She was thirty years old with a history of mental illness, divorced, and was unable to hold down a job. On that day, she snapped, and for whatever reason walked into that school and did what she did.

On one of our last live shots, the police announced she was dead. It appeared she was holding a family hostage, and when they made a break for it, she struggled with a twenty year old man, wounded him, went into another room in the house, and swallowed a bullet from her own gun.

That was that. The hell one person caused this small community would never be forgotten. The ensuing days brought every angle on a story you could possibly imagine. Psychologists, law enforcement experts, and school board presidents, all littered the airwaves with speculation. The story went on for days, but it was too real for me.

I was there to cover the funeral of the little eight-year-old boy.

It was a gray, cold, rainy day. In the silence of the procession, I watched a father carry his son's casket into the church. This was the second time in my life I'd seen such a sight, and this one was equally unnerving.

I kept hearing people say that this had to be his time. God must have had a plan, but I kept thinking, what kind of plan is that? A kid gets up in the morning, kisses his mom goodbye, goes to school, and gets killed. There were hundreds of people at this funeral, and everyone appeared to be thinking the same thing: How could such a thing happen?

\* \* \* \* \*

One day, I got a call from our news desk that some type of emergency was occurring at a nuclear power plant in Braidwood, Illinois. My instructions were to meet our soundman, Sal, and reporter Steve Hanley in the shop. It seemed a little odd to me that Sal was coming because we rarely used soundmen anymore, but I went with the flow. We drove to Meig's field, which was a lakefront launching pad for helicopters and small aircraft at the time. The three of us hopped into a helicopter for my first-ever chopper ride.

Our pilot was a three-time decorated Vietnam veteran named Burt who was known for bravery under fire. Amongst news people, he was a legendary figure. I heard that he once landed on a rooftop to pick up an order of ribs.

Steve and Sal were extremely happy that Burt was operating the helicopter. Even these old flying veterans were a little leery about the uncertainty of the aircraft, but they both agreed if anyone could keep it up in the air, it was Burt. As we were getting ready to take off, Sal extended the seat belt as far as it would go, wrapped it around my waist, then gaffer taped the buckle part, so it wouldn't come undone.

"What the fuck is going on?" I asked.

The copter started to lift off, and the engine noise drowned out everything, so Sal motioned for me to grab a headset. I could hear him almost laughing through the speakers.

"When we get to the nuclear plant," he said. "We'll pull back the door and you'll stand out on the skid, one leg in one leg out. I'm here to hold you and make sure you don't fall out."

Through the headsets, Burt and Steve were laughing. I must have had a terrified look on my face.

"Don't worry, buddy," Burt proudly boasted, "You'll be fine, haven't lost anyone yet,"

We soared over rooftops and neighborhoods, leaving the congestion of the city behind. We gained altitude over the suburbs, and soon we were in wide-open country with nothing but miles and miles of farmland in front of us.

"We're about three minutes away," Burt said, so Sal reached across me and slid the side door open. The engine noise inside of the chopper was escalated tenfold with the addition of the roaring wind from the open door.

I slowly placed my size twelve shoe on the skid, right leg out, left leg in. Sal had a shit-eating grin on his face. He grabbed the belt and positioned himself where he had some leverage in case he had to pull me in. As we approached the nuclear plant we could see ambulances heading through the front gate. I firmed myself against the opening of the copters doorway, and started videotaping. Steve told me what shots he would like via the headset.

After about ten minutes of hovering and taking in the limited activity happening on the ground, Burt told me what was next.

"I'm going to circle the plant to get us some quality shots of the entire facility," he said. "But be careful. I'll be going in a big loop. Be sure to look away from the camera from time to time, or you'll get vertigo, and you'll get dizzy quickly."

I gave him an understanding nod as if I knew what he was talking about, and off we went. Burt went into a circle pattern around the outside of the two big cooling towers. I was leaning against the frame of the open door, holding the camera steady as a rock. It was a hell of a nice shot.

Unfortunately, I had disregarded Burt's advice, and I didn't look up. I started to get very lightheaded and somewhat disoriented. I finally pulled my face away from the camera and tried to let the swirling wind revive me.

That was a futile attempt because the next thing I knew we were violently slammed to the left. The jolting was so hard I used my left hand to reach for Sal, leaving only my right hand inside the strap near the lens to hold the camera. That was a lot of weight to hold with only my right arm. I could feel the gravity pulling the camera almost over my head. I regained movement with my left hand and pulled the camera back to my shoulder.

Lights were flashing, and everything you can imagine was

beeping. We were violently thrown to our right, and the camera wrenched the shit out of my arm. I dropped it at my feet and now concentrated on purely surviving. I looked at Sal, and that smug look he had on his face earlier had been wiped clean. He looked scared, which scared me even more.

Burt was fighting to straighten us out of what seemed to be the beginning of a free fall. I just braced myself as we were thrown from side to side. Through the headsets came the shrill screams of what seemed to be a woman's voice on helium as someone was smashing her toes with a sledgehammer.

Sal and I looked at each other and realized neither of us were screaming. We focused our attention on the front of the copter. Burt was fighting the throttle of the floundering aircraft so we both knew he wasn't the screamer either. Then we looked at Steve. He had his arms in the air.

"We are going down!" he squealed. "Straighten us out! Do something, Burt! Do something!"

"Calm down, you fucking pussy," Sal yelled. "Stop scream-ing!"

Steve swung in our direction.

"We're going to fucking crash!" he squealed.

The copter was still swinging like a pendulum, Burt was fighting like a mad man, and we were losing altitude. I started to believe that soon I'd be getting in line to see if I made the grade for entrance to heaven or the odds-on favorite, hell. Dials were spinning, sensors were flashing, alarms were beeping, and the wind was whistling throughout the cabin. This may sound strange, but my palms stopped sweating, and a calm came over me. I was as ready as someone with short notice could be to die. Sal was relentless on Steve. He was yelling at him so much it got to the point that I blocked him out. His mouth was moving, but I heard nothing.

Soon the dropping feeling went away. We were still swinging from side to side, but not so aggressively. The dials weren't spinning so badly, and the alarms stopped beeping. We slowly started leveling off. Steve stopped his whining, and I could feel my legs and arms again. Sal looked at me and smiled. Burt had done it. He had pulled us out of a tailspin caused by the down draft near the cooling towers. The veteran pilot pulled us out of what appeared to be an almost certain bad ending to a simple assignment.

As we headed over an open field, Steve started screaming again.

"Set this thing down now," he screamed. "Set it down now!"

"Shut up you, pussy," Sal screamed back. "We're not setting down until we get back to Chicago."

Burt listened to Sal and kept flying back to the city. I remember staring out the chopper's open door at the farmland as we passed through at a high rate of speed and realizing I was going to live another day.

When Steve demanded to have the chopper land immediately again, Sal and I said it together.

"Shut the fuck up."

Burt gave us a thumbs up, and back home we went. When we landed, Steve hopped out of the aircraft, ran across the tarmac, and straight into a cab.

What a pussy.

# Chapter

 **STORIES OF DAYS GONE BY**

One afternoon, I found myself sitting in the shop, looking at the pictures on the walls of all the people who have worked there.

"What the fuck you doing, man?" Willie said, jolting me out of my daze.

"Just looking at some pictures," I said.

"Man, if these walls could speak you'd hear some crazy shit."

He sat down on a chair and sported an ear-to-ear smile. Willie was a man happy in his own skin. He was nearing the end of his career. He had seen and done it all and just wanted to laugh and enjoy the time he had left with his friends.

"It's been a beautiful ride," he said. "I saw the world on NBC's dime, worked with the best of the best, and laughed the whole time."

This job has a way of forming close relationships that are hard to describe. You bond under pressure, and you bond working side by side. That bond is life-long. That's certainly how I felt about Willie. He challenged me, made me think, and pushed my buttons until I realized he was playing me all along.

"Remember that day we worked together with Karen Monroe?" I asked.

"The travel agent double-billing story?" he said with a grin.

"Yeah, but that's not the part I remember," I said. "It was the drive there. Somehow we got on the subject of Jackie Onassis, and Karen said Jackie had a deal with Aristotle to participate in an arranged marriage. She said that Jackie got the lifestyle and money, and he got the prestige of being with her. Remember what you said?"

"I believe I said," Willie laughed, "'Are you trying to tell me the man never banged her?'"

"Yup," I laughed. "Karen said there was no way Jackie would ever have sex with that man, and you said…"

"No man would give some broad millions of dollars," Willie remembered, "and I don't give a fuck who she is, and not get any sex. No man."

"You got so pissed off," I reminded him.

It really was something to behold. Willie jammed on the brakes after that conversation, the car swerved to one side of the street, and a cab behind us hit his brakes just in time to avoid ramming into our rear. The cabbie laid on the horn until Willie hopped out and shot him a look. The cabbie drove around us quickly and left us with a token of his affection, his finger, while Willie opened the back door of our car, leaned in, and told Karen in a firm voice to get the fuck out of our car.

Karen was totally taken aback, and looked at Willie.

"You can't be serious," she said. "We have a story to cover."

"I'm not joking, Karen," Willie said. "I'm the head of this crew, and we're not working with someone so stupid and naïve. Get out!"

Her eyes started to well up with tears, and she started to shake.

"Q, can you help me, please?" she asked in a trembling

voice. "I don't understand this."

"Sorry, Karen, I can't," I said. "Willie runs the show."

It was the only response I could give because I didn't understand it either.

Karen slid across the seat and out the open door. Willie closed her door, got back behind the wheel, dropped the car in drive, and sped off. As soon as we were out of view he smiled.

"I know you think I'm nuts," he said, "but I'm just teaching our girl a life lesson."

Willie turned right at the first corner, then after taking two more rights, we were right back where we left her. Karen was still standing there and looking very out of sorts. Our car approached her, the window slowly lowered, and her eyes met ours.

"Get your white ass in here," Willie yelled.

"What is wrong with you?" Karen pleaded as she slowly approached the car. "Why would you do that to me?"

"Just get in," Willie said, very calmly this time.

Karen got into the backseat, and we drove for a couple blocks in silence. When there was finally a break in traffic, Willie turned around to face Karen.

"My father always said," Willie began, "try to help your friends when you see they are in trouble, or they are making a big mistake. Are we friends, Karen?"

"I thought we were," she said, "but you just kicked me to the curb. You're an asshole."

"I just saved you a ton of embarrassment," Willie said with a smile. "If you'd told that story to a couple of less compassionate guys, they'd have given you a lifetime's worth of shit. Karen, there is no way in the world a man would give a woman millions of dollars and not get laid. We can't let you walk this earth so naïve."

Karen was dumbfounded and stunned.

"You put me through that so you could belittle and upset me because I believed two people had an arrangement to have a sexless marriage?"

"Exactly," Willie said proudly.

At least a minute of silence passed. I slowly turned toward the backseat and locked eyes with Karen.

"You buy this bullshit too?" she demanded from me.

I just smiled at her.

"Assholes," she muttered.

After Willie and I relived that story, a few other guys entered the room, and one by one they pulled up a chair around Willie and me. It was story time, and my friend was the host. A voice from the back shouted out a request.

"Remember that story about Jack and the Mafia?"

The room fell silent. Harold, a long-time cameraman who was about to retire, took the floor.

"You guys have to know about this one," he said. "You know, the reporter they fired last year–Jack Meyers? He was a good reporter and a fearless bastard. They finally got rid of him because he stormed into a hospital room, thinking a politician was there, when it turned out to be an eighty-year-old woman recovering from a colon operation."

After the laughter died down, Harold regained control of the room.

"Now, fellas, you can take this one to the bank, I was there, and this is how it all happened. About five years ago we were covering the funeral of big-time mob boss, Johnny De Paully.

He was an old guy in his nineties, ran the whole mob show for a while. They put the media up on a hill overlooking the service. We were up there for quite some time watching the heads of all the different families show up, and it was driving Jack crazy because he wanted to interview them, and we couldn't leave our spot. Anyway, long story short, the service starts, and I looked over, and Jack was pacing back and forth, back and forth. Jack pointed down at four guys standing at the foot of the hill we're on, talking amongst themselves. I asked them who they were. Jack screamed—'Are you kidding me!'"

Our whole shop was silent. Harold had everyone's attention.

"It was Frankie somebody," Harold continued. "I can't remember his last name. Jack rattled off the names of the other three guys; God only knows who they were. Jack was almost ready to explode. He turned to me and Sal here, and said, 'We're going down there and talk to them!'"

Harold was now laughing as he told the story. Sal laughed along.

"I believe, and you can quote me on my response, I said – 'Fuck you, we go nowhere.' Jack was so angry; he was speechless. Then Sal came up with a great idea. He had a ton of microphone cable in the car and said he could string it all together, slap a microphone on it, and let Jack go down the hill and talk to them, while he shot everything from where we were."

"Jack couldn't get his hands on the microphone fast enough,"

Sal said, adding his two cents to the story. "There must have been a hundred feet of cable, and I think we used every inch."

"He made it right to the point where the bad guys were

standing," Harold continued. "Fucking Jack looked right up at me to make sure I was rolling before he asked Frankie, the mobster a question. He was out of breath from going down the hill, and Jack asked the man if he had anything to do with some murder of a federal judge in the late seventies. The mobster looked left, then right, took a step back, and then kicked Jack right square in the nuts."

Harold was laughing and very animated as kept on with the story.

"Guys, you know that sound, the sound of something popping, like when a boxer catches another fighter with a right hook directly in the stomach, and he's drained of all the air in his body. We all heard the sound of Jack's nuts heading into his throat."

It took a few seconds for the sound of laughing to die down in the shop before Harold could finish his story.

"Anyway, the three other mobsters formed a small circle around Jack and started putting the boots to his now deflated lifeless body. A good minute of tap dancing on Jack, and the boys slowly walked away. They didn't care who saw them. The police were at a distance and never even looked in Jack's direction. The little skirmish never disturbed a word of the nearby service. Sal and I were somewhat troubled by what we saw, but Jack was acting like such an asshole we just figured it was poetic justice. The funniest part of the whole thing was watching Jack slowly crawling up the hill, covered in dirt, his face white as a ghost. Every movement he made was accompanied by a painful moaning sound."

Harold just shook his head, laughing. The small group wanted more.

"You guys all remember Jill, don't you?" Willie said smiling, "Loved that woman."

The room fell silent at Willie's mention of her name. I knew her but not like some of these guys, who considered her family. Jill Presley was a strong-willed woman who started her career when television first started. By the time I got there, she was at the end of her game. Jill was black and white before things went color. Jill never married. The job was her life, and we were her family. She wore thick glasses, had a gruff deep voice caused by a lifetime of smoking, and had a heart of gold.

Of course, just because we all respected her, didn't mean that she wasn't going to get screwed with from time to time, and she did.

My first encounter with Jill was again courtesy of Willie. NBC had a policy that when we were sent to take a lunch hour, we had to inform the news desk where we were dining. Even though we had pagers, the company liked to know exactly where we were. One day, Willie and I got sent on an unexpected trip to New York City with the investigative unit to film documents and location shots. Willie dialed our newsroom number and told Jill to put us out to lunch at the Carnegie Deli.

"Why did you do that?" I asked. "We're out of town. She doesn't need to know where we're eating."

"You'll see," Willie said.

When we returned from our east coast trip the next day and walked into the newsroom, this deep foggy voice bellowed at us.

"Willie, you fucking jerk," she screamed. "I was looking for you two assholes all afternoon; no one told me you were in New York. I didn't know the Carnegie Deli wasn't in Chicago!"

When we turned to see her, we saw this older woman in the corner of the room giving us the finger. Willie gave me a little push, and we headed toward her.

"I was looking for you clowns for hours," Jill said. "I wanted you to cover a fire in one of the suburbs. I felt like an asshole when I found out you were out of town."

That was how I met her. Jill held her hand out to me and introduced herself when we got closer to her.

"Watch out for this one," she said, pointing to Willie. "He screws with me all the time, but I love him. Gets me good sometimes, too."

They hugged, and all was forgiven.

But that wasn't the most famous Jill story and not the story that everyone wanted to tell that day in the shop. We all remembered another story—our favorite Jill story of all time.

The two tallest buildings in Chicago are the John Hancock to the north of the downtown, and the Sears Tower (now Willis Tower) to the south of the city. All the television stations assembled "receive sites" on these two roofs for microwave transmissions. We would send our signal from our live trucks to either the Sears or the Hancock receive sites, then the signal would go from there to the transmission area of the station. There were two settings on the trucks to transmit that signal: two-gigahertz or seven-gigahertz. It was just a matter of flicking a different switch.

Part of the job of the desk was to tell the crew the setting and receive site. Well, Jill didn't quite understand this concept, so she turned to her pal Willie. Willie took advantage of the poor woman's lack of technology and hearing and told her the settings were two or seven clitahertz. At the time, we still communicated with the news desk only by two-way radio, so all of the crews heard every transmission.

Every day, around live shot time, the call went over the radio asking if it was two or seven, and was it Sears or Hancock?

"It's two clitahertz," the gravelly voiced Jill would say.

For all of us in the field, no matter what we were doing, we'd huddle around our radios and laugh like it was the first time we ever heard it. When guys really wanted to play, they'd turn it up a notch.

"My," they'd answer.

There was always a silence before she'd reply.

"My clitahertz?"

That was the home run for us immature little kids. God, we'd laugh. Our fun was ruined when a new manager filled Jill in on the phrase's true meaning. She didn't speak to Willie for months, until he bought her a whiskey sour at a party one night, when all was forgiven.

Jill was a wealth of knowledge and kindness, someone who looked out for her friends. Her friends were there for her, too. As years passed, she started to falter in her job, and Jill retired. Shortly after that, she passed away. We were her only survivors.

When we finished telling the story about Jill, all of us sat back in our chairs.

To get up every morning and be excited about coming to work was a rare and unusual thing, and that's how I felt about that place and the people I worked with every day.

I loved these guys.

I loved the work we did.

I didn't want it to ever end.

# Chapter

# THE END IS NEAR, THE END IS HERE

Rumors were swirling around all the NBC owned and operated stations that some serious layoffs were coming. Despite what General Electric said about not changing anything when they took over NBC, their real plan was to go lean and mean, which meant cutbacks and layoffs. It also meant yours truly was in some serious trouble. I was number one hundred-forty out of one hundred-eighty three guys on the seniority list.

One day as I walked into the station, Mike Workmen, (a production manager) pulled me aside.

"Chuck," he said, "we just had a manager's meeting, and they told us the company was going to be eliminating close to eighty technical jobs in the next few months."

It was as if someone had kicked me squarely in the stomach. I was stunned and speechless.

"I'm breaking the golden rule of managers by telling you this," he said, "but I like you, and I want you to have as much notice as possible. I'm not sure when the layoffs are coming, but they're coming."

This was an unusual time in the business. Broadcast companies were starting to beat up on the unions. They'd lay off a guy then bring him back to fill the same job without his benefits. People were scared, and I'd be the first to admit, I was front and center in the frightened department.

When the layoff dates were finalized, the company decided to offer buyout packages to the older employees. That still wasn't enough to save us newer guys. I was given a one-month notice. The company announced they were going to put the guys with the most seniority on the streets, even though they'd never done the job before. We were essentially training them to do our jobs.

With just a few weeks left in my tenure, I was approached by an NBC Network News producer about helping out with a piece they were doing about Chicago gangs. The producer wanted to pull me out of local news for one night and do a ride along with a Chicago police gang unit. Other crews had been riding along with a couple of gang crime officers for a week and had come up empty as far as videoing any actual gang activity.

They had interviews, and night and daytime shots in the can, but they were giving it one last attempt to get some live, on-camera gang interaction. Without it, the piece seemed doomed to ever see the light of day. So there I was, as the afternoon fell into darkness, quietly sitting with my camera in the back of an unmarked squad car.

My escorts were two of Chicago's finest, Officers Rick and James. They had ten and fourteen years on the job, respectively, and I could tell they had no desire to baby-sit me for the evening. Both officers downplayed the prospect of getting into any type of a dangerous situation that night.

"It's not warm enough," Rick kept repeating. "The assholes kill each other when it's hot."

We drove through the Hispanic neighborhoods, street by street, enjoying the music and the smell of the food. Countless bad guys stared at us, and each one knew we were the man.

After only one stop for a churros and a short bout of indigestion, we were close to calling it a night when the call came. Shots had been fired in a nearby park. We made it to the park's entrance at a break neck pace, and Officer Rick made a move I had never seen before. He shut off the headlights and accelerated. He was doing at least sixty miles an hour through the grassy areas of the park, guided only by the faint glow of the streetlights scattered throughout the park. These guys had been here before. This was no game to them. Officer James turned around and faced me.

"When we get out," he said, "stick close and don't turn on that fucking light, no matter what. Got it? No light."

I nodded back to him, even though he couldn't see me in the dark.

"There he is," Rick shouted.

Under the glow of one lone light at the park's edge in an alleyway, we saw a man's body. We stopped with a jarring halt, the doors were thrust open, and suddenly the three of us were standing over a Hispanic male. He was still alive, but barely.

I was struggling from being slightly out of breath from the adrenaline rush I was experiencing. I had never seen such a thing, someone was dying right before my eyes. My mind started wandering. I was going back to places I thought I'd forgotten, people I hadn't seen in years, places I'd been, and never will be again. My head was elsewhere. The camera was pointed at him, but I wasn't rolling.

I was frozen, stunned by his stare, I couldn't video his last moments on earth. His eyes slowly started tearing up. His glare seemed to go directly to my soul. The man needed help, but I couldn't save him. All I could do was record his demise.

I steadied the camera and hit the record button. The counter read a minute twenty, and then he was gone.

March 5th, 1993.

I watched a person die.

The producers of the show reviewed the tape, and the piece never aired. They said it wasn't what they needed. Apparently they had some kind of vision for the story, and they hadn't bargained on coming face to face with death.

I would never again see what happened that night, yet, I still see it all the time.

I see it in my mind.

\* \* \* \* \*

My remaining workdays at NBC were a blur. On my last day, with my belongings in hand, I quietly said goodbye to the people who happened to be around, took one last look around, and went out the front door. There was a slight breeze bouncing off my face as I stood outside, feeling like I'd never see a dear friend or an old lover again.

"You've got a job for life," the Chief Engineer once told me, and that was ringing in my ears. Of course it wasn't true, but at least I had a severance check to live on, a great resume tape, and I was leaving with ton of wonderful memories.

# Chapter

## 17  A NEW ERA BEGINS

Shortly after leaving NBC, I was contacted by a local independent station. They just happened to be expanding their local news shows and needed to add more staff. I realized how fortunate I was in finding work so quickly in the city I loved, doing a job I truly enjoyed.

This station had been airing one news show for years at night, but now they wanted to get in the game by adding a morning and noon newscast. They were trying to get to a place where the big three networks had been for a while, but it was going to take some time. Their strategy was to be edgy and hip and give Chicago a different approach to the news.

My first day there, I was greeted by the assignment manager Paul. He was in a sweat soaked panic.

"There's so much to do," he said, "and not enough people to do the work. Are you comfortable shooting?"

"I'm a cameraman," I explained to him.

That day I worked a fifteen and a half hour day, and for the rest of that week it seemed like I worked unlimited overtime. In fact, it was so much work I had to argue with a desk person to at least let me have five minutes to get to the personnel department, so I could fill out the proper forms to receive a check on payday.

This newsroom was the Ellis Island of Chicago newsrooms. Everyone there was a refugee from another station, a victim of layoffs, firings, or expired contracts. Each person had a story, and each person was looking for a second chance.

The general manager of the station was a woman in her mid-thirties named Cindy. She had been the head of a promotions department at another network when she was recruited to run her own station. This was a pretty radical move at the time. Most GMs were hardened male news veterans who ran through several stations and a few secretaries on their way to a market like Chicago. Our owners figured that adding a younger woman would bring a fresh perspective and new ideas to attract younger viewers.

I got to meet the new GM in the newsroom a week or so after I started. She was a good-looking, confident individual.

"I understand you came from NBC," she said, extending her hand, "and I've heard nothing but good things about you. Welcome aboard."

"Thank you," I said. "I have heard nothing but good things about you too."

It was the only thing that popped into my vacant mind. It was 6am, too damn early, and I was wondering what someone who ran a television station was doing at the office that early. After we exchanged pleasantries, she stood there smiling. I smiled back; it was one of those uneasy moments.

"Would you please grab your camera and give me a ride to Union Station?" she finally said.

"Sure," I replied, promising to meet her in the parking garage in five minutes.

I couldn't quite figure what this was all about. Union Station is the busiest commuter train station in Illinois. Thousands of suburbanites come through there daily on the way to their jobs in the city.

"Wondering what we're going to see at Union Station?" she asked, she was beaming.

"Very much," I said lying through my teeth.

"I had an extra ten thousand dollars in my budget, so I had coffee mugs made up to advertise the morning show, and as we speak they are being handed out to commuters."

"Great idea," I shot back, adjusting my vagina.

Shortly after she started at the station, she had launched a three-hour morning show with three different solo anchors in three different hours. It was different. They had a futuristic looking set, with a giant logo in the background, surrounded with flashy graphics. The ratings were dismal. This coffee mug idea was her chance to boost those ratings.

Once we got to the train station, I grabbed my camera to record this historic event, and off we went. The walk took quite a while throughout the underground hallways of the train station, before we came upon three criminal looking characters opening up cartons of mugs. After they opened the boxes, they just stood back and let people exiting the trains take as many as they wanted. It was a feeding frenzy, and these three goofs didn't give a shit. One lady must have taken six mugs, and the only thing stopping her from taking more was the line pushing her aside. I lifted my camera and started to record. I thought this could be a major news story, people trampled for mugs, and we had caused it.

Just a few seconds after I started videotaping, Cindy grabbed my arm and asked me to stop. As I lowered the camera, she walked away from me and toward the box of mugs. She grabbed one, looked at me, and motioned for me to leave.

It was silent in the car ride back until she broke the ice.

"Can I get your honest opinion?" she asked.

"Sure," I replied.

"From what you saw, do you think I made a smart move?"

She literally stuck the mug in my face, and I looked it over. I was trying to buy time before my answer.

"The mug looks good," I lied.

It was all white with a goofy looking logo that said CMN. She adjusted herself in the front seat, faced me head on, and pressed me for an answer.

"Be honest," she said.

I was watching my career flash before my very eyes, but I answered anyway.

"Well, to be honest," I said, "the mug is lacking as far as advertising your product goes. It just says CMN on it, not Chicago Morning News, and not everyone knows what that is. It doesn't say the time or what station it's on, and as far as the train station goes, all those people who took a mug work at the time the show is on and will never watch."

That warm feeling came over me again. What was wrong with me? Why wasn't I smart enough to shut my mouth? What was I expecting? That she was going to smile at me and tell me I was so right, and ask me to be her right hand man to help run the station with her? Why didn't I just kiss her ass?  She's a nice woman. Why screw with her?  I waited her response for what seemed like hours, but it was probably only a matter of seconds. She forced a smile.

"Thanks," she said.

From that day forward, on the rare occasions I saw her, she was always polite and never showed any ill will. I thought that was very classy; not holding it against a cameraman who told her idea was a piece of shit.

\* \* \* \* \*

## A SNAPSHOT IN TIME/1994/NICOLE SIMPSON'S MURDER

OJ stayed in a hotel on Cumberland Ave. right off the Kennedy expressway the night Nicole was murdered. We heard that he took a walk in a wooded area behind the hotel that evening. A theory was floating around that he had dumped the murder weapon, a knife, amongst the trees and brush. We were all sent out there the next day to take shots of the hotel and the police as they searched for the weapon. (To this day, I consider that a bit ridiculous. Airport security back then wasn't as rigid as today, but still, carrying a knife on a plane?) An assignment person from one of the other local stations supposedly sent an intern to the crime scene after the police left to continue his own search for the weapon, figuring the police didn't know what they were doing and Joe College was going to get the big scoop. Needless to say, that move was a giant step backwards in the career of that assignment person.

The morning show was billed as state of the art television. It was hip and cool, fast paced and edgy, but it didn't work in

Chicago. Whether they wanted to believe it or not, Chicago was a meat and potatoes town. Chicago viewers only wanted competent people delivering a good product, not bullshit. The critics gave it props for attempting to be different, but in the same breath, they made it clear that the competition had nothing to worry about.

The brains behind Chicago's most un-talked about show, was a guy named Ron Foremen. This guy was an interesting sort. He was a short, hyperactive, mostly bald guy that sported a ponytail he constantly touched or twirled around. He dressed like shit, had a constant body funk, spoke very fast, and always smiled. He was proud of the show and had faith one day it would rise through the ashes and conquer all of television.

But Ron was such a paranoid soul that he hired his own little group of 'yes' men. They were a crew of smiling know nothings he must have befriended at his last place of employment (probably Target.) They were all slimy little fucks, but one stood out as chief knucklehead, the ringleader named Garth. He was the spitting image of Hoss Cartwright from the television show Bonanza, only with curly hair.

Garth was Ron's right hand man and was known for making incredibly stupid executive decisions, such as paying thousands of dollars for a piano rental for a four minute segment with a nobody singer. Another move at the top of his resume was a three-hour "Battle of the Bands" on Christmas Day. That's right, Christmas Day. He was also the brains behind a beachwear segment, where the news talent dressed in swimsuits for the whole show live from Oak Street Beach...on a chilly Chicago autumn day.

One of my favorite things Ron implemented for the show

was his insistence that all video we shot had to be on an angle, MTV style. No matter what we did, it had to be at an angle. Fires, sporting events, even weather shots; every frame was slanted. There were cameramen who came from different stations such as me with years of experience, and we all thought this nut was out of his mind. Some refused to go along with this madness, and that infuriated the pony-tailed visionary.

One day we were all summoned up to Ron's office, where he talked to all of us as if we were little children.

"Slanted video is the backbone of this morning show," he told us.

He then walked over to a television set, grabbed a videotape of MTV reruns with his greasy little hands, and slapped it in the VCR.

"Study this," he said and left the room, closing the door behind him.

I looked around the room at the other guys. Everyone was stunned. This asshole was crazy and getting crazier. The station poured tons of money into the show and got no results. It was wearing on management, but most of all, it was getting to our man Ron. According to rumors, he was sleeping in his office every night, putting in twenty-hour days, searching desperately for the solution to his ratings woes.

One day he was overcome with a stroke of brilliance. He came up with a segment we could tease all morning to hook the viewers and make them stay glued to their television sets. This three-minute miracle was to be called: "Shoes."

He walked around with the swagger that say a Francis Ford Coppola may have had after the screening of Godfather as he announced it to us.

"All hands on deck," the ponytailed genius said, as he told us all about his brilliant idea. Because he was handcuffed by budget constraints, Ron was forced to use someone in house to star in this great new segment, but after carefully and meticulously weeding through what little he had to choose from, he had discovered the vehicles for his brilliance. One was a pale-skinned blonde girl with high hair. Her name was Danielle. The other was a stunning, well-built black girl named Samantha.

"These two," he said proudly, "will go into shoe stores, talk about the latest footwear fashion, and try on different shoes."

It was greeted with the kind of enthusiasm you might have expected, but that didn't deter the pony-tailed one. It was a taped segment. So, once a week Ron pulled three cameramen out of covering local news to invade local shoe stores. The shooting went on for hours with these two young dimwits talking about footwear, while being egged on by their director Ron.

"Genius!" he would say. "Way to sell it!"

After countless hours of footage, endless takes and missed cues, the production was taken into editing where it was given the full treatment with effects and even a soundtrack. Once that was finished, it was given countless hours of promotion.

"Shoes" was to be the last segment on a Wednesday morning. Ron was beaming like a proud father in the control room and boasting to everyone that this was his ticket to syndication. He couldn't wait for the reviews to roll in. But the next day the local critics never mentioned a thing in their newspaper columns, and viewer response was very slight. By slight, I mean only one person sent in an opinion via email, simply stating, "The blonde dresses like a whore."

Ron was sensing the noose tightening on his career, and he

had no more new concepts on the horizon, so he decided that "Shoes" just needed a kick in the ass, creatively. Ron told the girls to give it more sex appeal. If the world can't see they're hot, then by God, we need to tell them they are. He pulled Danielle aside and gave her a pep talk, then gave me my instructions.

"I want a tight shot of her as she says her closing line. And when Samantha steps in, I want them both in the shot. Got it?"

I nodded. So Danielle got ready for her big line of lines. She held up a shoe, stared right into the lens of the camera, and delivered it.

"These shoes are hot," she said, "but we're hotter, just watch and find out how hot we can be."

I looked through my viewfinder and saw the two of them go cheek-to-cheek and mug for the camera. In the corner of the room I could hear Ron applauding wildly. In his tiny mind, he had just struck gold.

By then, the morning show was around nine months into its run and dying fast. The ratings stayed flat-lined, and the salesmen couldn't give it away. Corporate was pressuring the GM, Cindy, to make a profit with this mess. We all know that shit runs downhill and it was running double time toward our boy, Ron.

More segments of "Shoes" were being churned out, and the public failed to respond. In a state of total panic, Ron thinned the herd; dumping Samantha and naming Danielle a solo act. This move failed to garner any movement in the numbers. It appeared the fat lady was about to sing. Now that his Hail Mary pass had been dropped, Ron decided he should concentrate on the other two hours and fifty-seven minutes of the show. In theory, the show was news oriented. But it had strayed from that into a gang-bang of entertainment, weather, and sports, presented by people who seemed uneasy presenting it.

In the final hours Ron dispatched his small group of unknown air talent into the community, ordering them to do stories that affected the typical Chicagoan, but his unknowns weren't from Chicago and didn't know what typical Chicagoans wanted. It was estimated that Chicago Morning News lost over a million dollars in operating costs with no results. Ron packed what little he had along with what was left of his integrity and left town.

The next few weeks were interesting to watch. Management brought in a new executive producer and renamed the morning show. They hired a new anchor team, and slowly but surely started picking off the remaining CMN air staff and Ron's unprotected flock of 'yes' men. Once intolerably arrogant, they now scurried like rats to their holes. The new staff hunted down Ron's rats and eliminated them one by one.

Only one seemed to escape the long arm of justice, for a brief period anyway. Garth brilliantly extended his shelf life for a while by coming in very early in the morning and leaving right when all the new managers came in to start their day. Truthfully, I think they just forgot about him until he sealed his own fate.

One morning, he was in the control room coordinating the morning live shots. Garth liked to talk to the guys in the field to let them know how much time they had between live shots, what phone line to dial in on. You know, busy work. On this morning, a live crew was at O'Hare Airport waiting for the arrival of the Archbishop Of Chicago, Joseph Cardinal Bernardin, who was returning from a conference of priests. They were experiencing a time crunch with the newly formatted show, so Garth was pressuring the crew to find the Cardinal and get him in front of the camera.

Time went by, and all they could see in the control room was a shot of the airport's arrival area. Garth was now beside himself, yelling at the crew. Getting no response back and unable to get a visual, he became more agitated and more vulgar. He finally saw the cameraman pass by the camera but still no Cardinal. This sent him into a fury.

"Get the fucking Cardinal in front of the motherfucking camera right now!" he screamed.

As soon as those words came out of his mouth, the Cardinal stepped in front of the camera. It seemed the cameraman had been off to the side putting the Cardinal's IFB in his ear, so he could hear the studio. The Cardinal definitely heard Garth's tirade.

Silence struck the entire control room. That stupid bastard said 'fuck' to a Cardinal. It appeared that our man Garth was not only a marked man with management, he now also had a one-way ticket straight to hell. The Cardinal showed a lot of class, graciously doing the live shot and never saying a word about what he heard.

The next day, management came in early and caught up with Garth. It was a fast and well-executed termination.

# Chapter  THE KING OF POP

Michael Jackson returned to his hometown of Gary, Indiana on a warm day in June. I pulled that assignment along with a field producer, Paul, who was a real character. He had a dry sense of humor and a vocabulary that was mostly comprised of "asshole" and "jag off." Our orders were to follow and try to talk to the "King of Pop" as he visited his original home and a local high school.

Once we pulled into the city limits of Gary, we were stunned by the number of crazed fans in attendance. Hundreds of onlookers were lined up for blocks near the Jackson family home (which, by the way, was located on Jackson Street). The police had put up six-foot fencing around most of the area, so only Michael and his entourage could have access to his childhood home. Paul and I somehow wedged our bodies between a pair of three hundred pound women smashed against the chain-linked fence.

I shot through the fence, chronicling the zoo before us. The crowd was comprised of black, white, Hispanic, young, and old people. At first it was a party atmosphere, but the crowd had become somewhat restless when a couple of squad cars broke through the frenzied throng, followed by a limousine.

Michael Jackson stepped out of the car, surrounded by a

wall of bodyguards and a guy holding an umbrella to protect him from the sun. Michael waved to the crowd, and the place went wild. The fence was shaking back and forth violently. Our three hundred pound friends were attempting to topple the chain link barrier.

Michael turned and waved in all directions, trying to acknowledge everyone in attendance. He and his entourage then entered the modest dwelling. The crowd became more excited. People were screaming and crying. Paul looked at me in disbelief. He shook his head and yelled so I could hear him.

"Don't these assholes have jobs?"

That was a good point. How could so many people show up here on a Wednesday morning? Paul and I slowly worked our way out of the crowd. We knew the high school was his next stop, so we decided to get in our car and get a head start to that location.

I was putting my camera away into the trunk of our car, when a young man probably no older than eighteen grabbed my arm. He had a crazed look in his eyes and a body odor that would stop an elephant stampede.

"Put me on television!" he demanded.

"Take a hike," I replied.

"Please," he begged. "I'm Michael's biggest fan! I want to tell the world what he did for me."

I shut the trunk with the camera in it, but I thought, what the hell, before he heads back to the trailer court I'll ask.

"All right pal, what did Michael do for you?"

He turned his back to me and lifted his shirt. Across his acne-riddled shoulders, Michael Jackson had written his name in magic marker. My yellow-toothed friend explained that he was going to have a tattoo made of the autograph.

"Take a picture of it!" he said.

"I don't think so," I replied.

The high school visit was way more organized. We actually got inside the auditorium, but because of security constraints we were convinced we'd never get close to the great one, let alone talk to him. We were there almost an hour before Michael and his entourage finally entered through a side door to thunderous applause from the packed room.

They had an entire program set up for the pop star, and he seemed to really enjoy it. Students gave speeches about how important the former Gary resident was and how he had influenced the world of music. The choir sang songs, and Michael received a football jersey with his name on it. Every time he spoke the place went nuts. From our vantage point I could barely get a shot of him. There were too many people.

Paul and I agreed that our only hope of getting a decent shot was to get him leaving the school. We exited the side door and stood next to his limousine, but his bodyguards pushed us away. By this time, we were pretty discouraged and ready to put Gary, Indiana in our rearview mirror. The crowds got bigger outside the school, waiting for his exit. The bodyguards formed a human barricade to keep his fans at bay, and Paul and I headed to our car. It was no use. We weren't going to get a shot of him.

As we were walking away, the crowd noise became deafening, and I turned around and looked. The bodyguards had everyone pressed up close to the school, but Michael and the man who held his umbrella for him were standing there, virtually unprotected, no more than fifty yards away. There wasn't a soul between us. It was go time, my only chance to get a clean picture of Michael Jackson. As I try to stealthily head toward him, I could hear my feet scraping the pavement with every step. Paul was a few feet behind me.

"Holy shit, holy shit," he whispered.

The camera was rolling and firmly on my shoulder as I got closer and closer. When I got about thirty feet away I slowed down. I was being overly conscious about making any kind of noise that might announce our presence and draw security toward us. By the time I was ten feet away, I still hadn't been noticed. Michael had his head down, signing a t-shirt, and his umbrella holder was facing in the opposite direction.

I had him perfectly in focus and was standing on his left side, no more than five feet away from him. I silently video-taped taped him for a good thirty seconds. As I was rolling, I got a real good look at him. His hands were boney and light skinned. He wore a black sweater with white patches on his shoulders. His hair was long and parted down the middle. I took a step closer and pulled my head away from the camera to get a closer look at his face. His nose was tiny and upturned. It didn't look real. I was fixated. It looked like it was made of putty. That's when I figured out why he had a guy holding an umbrella for him on a sunny day. I think Michael was afraid the sun would melt his face if he became exposed to it for any length of time.

He didn't look human. He looked like a mannequin. I inched even closer. He still had his head down signing autographs, so I leaned even closer. Suddenly, he looked up and lunged at me with a magic marker. He stopped the felt tipped instrument a fraction of an inch from my camera lens and shrieked.

"EWW, you're too close."

That's when I felt a sharp pain in my lower back and an incredible amount of pain in my shoulder and neck area. His hired band of thugs were showing Paul and I the fast way to exit a school parking lot. They shoved, pushed, and taunted us away from him, and I got one last glance of "The King of Pop" as his bodyguards finally bid us farewell.

He had a sadistic smile on his face.

His eyes sent the message, "Take that asshole."

## A SNAPSHOT IN TIME/1996/PRINCESS DIANA VISITS CHICAGO

Princess Diana took tours of the city almost every day of her visit. I was at Cook County Hospital's emergency room with a buddy of mine. We were the pool camera for that day's tour of the inside of the hospital. I remember her slowly walking by everyone, shaking hands and smiling. Everyone was going crazy; a barrage of camera flashes nearly blinded me. She eventually made it toward the end of the line where we were. Stopping and smiling, she said "Hello." Rarely in my life have I been speechless, but in this case, the best I could do was smile back at her. As she turned and walked away, my buddy finally regained his composure and said to me rather loudly, "She's smoking hot!" I know she heard him, because she turned her head slightly, and I could make out a slight smile on her face. He was right on the money. She was smoking hot.

# Chapter

# THE CLOWN AND
# THE CORPSE

Chicago has a rich history as the epicenter of organized crime. Spend any time in Chicago, and you'll quickly get familiar with the names of mobsters that were heads of the local families. There was "Jimmy the Man," "The Gumba," "Big Tuna," "The Ant," "Doves," "The Lackey," and my favorite "The Clown."

Joey "The Clown" Lombardo was a chart topper on the FBI's most wanted list for most of his life. Joey was somewhat of a cult figure because he eluded the law for several years. At the age of seventy-six, he was still on the lam. He was a street-smart alleged ruthless killer known for his eccentric ways, but he blended in with the heartbeat of the local area. Local law enforcement couldn't track him because they couldn't catch something they couldn't see.

The longer he eluded the law, the more airtime he got on the local stations. He became a Robin Hood to the locals. The feds counter-attacked by putting his resume out for all to see. Lombardo started out as a poor street kid in the 1950's, became a jewel thief, went on to be a juice loan collector, a hit man, and eventually the capo of the Grand Avenue crew, with thirty soldiers at his disposal. But to the people of his community, he was one of them for better or worse, and it seemed to be an unbreakable bond.

As time passed, Joey tempted fate by sending a letter to a judge with his surrender terms and a suggestion for a very low bond. On top of that, he wanted a separate trial from the rest of his codefendants. He then signed the letter "Joey Lombardo, An Innocent Man."

That appeared to really piss off the feds. They turned up the heat up on him, and on a cold January day, the law finally got their man. It was front-page news on the newsstands and the top story on every television station. A couple of days after the arrest, I was assigned, along with reporter Don Planter, to go to the near west side of Chicago to talk to people who had encountered Joey. This area housed a small pocket of homes and Italian businesses, surrounded by Hispanic and black gangs. In all the years he was on the lam the tight-knit Italian community was never breached by those gangs, largely because of Joey's influence.

When we got there, it was like entering a movie set. Steam was rising from the sewer grates that lined the brick-paved street. The delis and grocery stores had neon "We're Open" lights in their windows but otherwise showed no sign of life. We were in an area untouched by outside influences. The streets had eyes, and they were fixed on us.

We traveled from business to business, house to house, stood shivering on street corners, and not one soul would speak to us. We passed by what we thought was a locked door belonging to a small corner pub, but as we passed, the door became slightly ajar.

"Try the Italian social club at the end of the block," a female voice instructed us, followed by the door slowly clicking shut.

We were an unwanted presence, and this appeared to be our last option. The building had no sign or name on it and needed desperately to have a paintbrush taken to it. We banged on the door repeatedly, and no one answered. Don turned the door-knob. It was open, so we ventured down a dimly lit hallway. As we got closer, we heard the faint sounds of a voice calling out numbers.

We walked directly into a smoke-filled, badly paneled room littered with folding chairs and card tables. To our surprise, we were instantly surrounded by a horde of blue-haired old ladies. They were piled three deep hovering around their bingo cards, but no one noticed us.

We made it to the head of the room before a young woman approached us.

"Can I help you?" she asked.

"We're here to do a story on Joey Lombardo," Don said.

The woman burst into laughter.

"They all loved the man in this community," she explained. "You won't hear an ill word about him here—that is if anyone will even speak to you at all."

We waited for a lull in the number calling, and I scanned the room looking for just one friendly face. It was a convention of grandmothers, and not one of them would make eye con-tact. When the eighty-plus year old number caller went into a coughing jag, Don seized the moment. He elevated his voice but was careful not to frighten the elderly crowd.

"Would anyone here like to talk to us about Joe Lombar-do?" he said. Silence fell over the room. Don shot me a look, then tried again. "We know that most of you know him. If you just talk about the good he's done in your community, that could be an asset to him."

He was greeted with complete silence other than the occasional creaking of a chair. They were all trained well. Not one woman was going to give up anything. It was an odd feeling, being stared down by a room full of hostile old women. When no one answered, we figured it was time to make our exit. The number caller regained her composure, and the game resumed.

On the way out, I made eye contact with a standard looking grandmother. Her eyes narrowed the more she looked at me. She was draped in gold jewelry, and her white hair was piled high.

She slowly lifted her right hand and motioned for me to come closer. I leaned forward through her force field of heavily applied perfume; again, she motioned for me to come closer yet. Her eyes narrowed even further. Glancing from left to right, she straightened herself in her chair, and with her eyes now wide open, she finally spoke.

"Why don't you shove that camera in your ass?"

I stepped back and kept my eyes locked onto hers. She was unwavering. This woman had some rage building up, and I was the recipient. I looked over at Don, and he was ready to burst into laughter. When I returned my eyes to the old lady, she was still glaring at me. I smiled at her, and only then did she drop her eyes back down to her bingo card.

\* \* \* \* \*

## A SNAPSHOT IN TIME/9-11-2001

I was on the west side of the city, waiting for another Michael Jordan basketball comeback. This time, he was going to play for Washington, but like always, we covered everything he did. I was standing outside talking to the guys in a live truck when the network cut in with a plane crash at the World Trade Center. We watched in the monitor, and as the anchors speculated how such a thing could happen, plane two went into the second tower. At that point, everything went up for grabs. Our radios and phones went off like crazy. Chicagoans gravitated to whatever televisions they could find, and the city's streets soon became empty. I was sent to United Airlines headquarters in case the airline held a press conference. I waited into the night, and they never did. But the thing that sticks in my mind the most is about that day was when a friend of mine called me, cursing a blue streak. It seemed that once his assignment desk found out the Sears Tower was another building the terrorists were targeting, they asked him to go there and set up the live truck in case something happened. I can still remember laughing with him as we tried to figure what kind of a person would ask him to set up where a plane was going to crash.

One hot summer night, I met up with a live truck and reporter on the city's North Side. The desk heard lots of police activity on the scanner. They weren't quite certain what was happening, but it sounded as if a dead body had been found.

The streets were lined with live trucks when I arrived, and television lights illuminated the whole block. The police had sealed off an entire city block, but their attention was focused primarily on a drain in the center of an alley. I set up my camera as close as the police would allow, and when I did, I saw two cops using two-by-fours like chopsticks in the sewage drain trying to fish something out.

People were watching this from roofs, porches, and fences. Little kids were perched on the shoulders of adults. It was hotter than hell, and this seemed to take their minds off the uneasiness of the night.

"What happened?" I asked the reporter Scott.

"A guy was out washing his car when he smelled a strong odor emanating from the sewage drain," he told me. "It took a while for the street and sanitation guys to pry off the drain cover, but when they did, they found a body stuffed inside the drain."

This person must have been really wedged down in there because the officers were struggling to get leverage to free the body. They were snorting and grunting in the hot and humid night, and every time they made a failed attempt, the onlookers heckled them. The desk was really on us for a live picture, and as I started to answer my radio, Scott grabbed my arm.

"Hold off on answering them," he said. "Let's make them wait. Let's run it right up to live shot time."

Scott hated the desk manager–and the feeling was mutual–but Scott was one of those veterans every newsroom had to have because he saw through the bullshit and knew how the job was done. The truck operator and I ran all the cables from the truck, and we were ready to go live in no time. The radio was dancing on my hip. The desk was calling every thirty-seconds.

I could hold out no longer, so I answered it.

"Where the fuck have you guys been?" the voice on the other end demanded.

"Relax!" I snapped back, "Do you have any idea how much shit we had to go through just to get situated out here? We'll be ready; don't worry."

Scott grabbed the microphone from my other hand, smiled, and nodded to me as if to say good job. Scott loved the game of busting balls. He thought that they never gave people in the field enough credit as far as knowing our jobs, and he was right. With two minutes to go, the director started talking to us in our earpieces.

"Chuck," he said, "we'd like you to start out on Scott then zoom into the area where the recovery is going on and hold the shot there."

Scott heard this and waved his arms into the camera, normally an attention getter.

"Better watch the time you spend on the drain," he advised. "That body could pop up at any moment, and it could be ugly."

"Thanks for that," the director said condescendingly. "We'll deal with it back here."

Scott stepped from camera range and winked at me. I smiled back at him. I knew what was going through his mind and what he hoped to accomplish. During the show's open, the director gave us a thirty-second cue. He then told Scott that he had only forty-five seconds on air. Scott smiled and nodded to the camera. The crowd around us got bigger and more vocal.

Scott leaned toward me.

"Getting loud out here," he said exaggeratedly. "Going to be tough to hear the director."

The anchor read the intro then threw it to Scott. From there Scott told the story of the man washing his car and how he smelled the odor coming from the sewer drain, which led us to the scene behind him. I zoomed past Scott and focused right on the opening of the sewer. Scott, now off camera, read his script with one eye on the officers. At that very moment they looked as if they were struggling quite a bit. Forty-five seconds expired and the director was calling for a wrap, but Scott kept talking, I stayed focused on the straining officers and the sewer. Scott knew he was off camera, and he smiled to me and kept speaking, at one point mentioning how loud it was.

The director was now screaming.

"Wrap!" he shouted. The camera was right on the sewer, and the officers were still struggling. Scott kept talking while the director kept shouting, "Wrap! Wrap it up!"

Then it happened. In one big surge, both officers pried the body free, and it literally sprang from the sewer onto the ground, making a big splat on the asphalt. People started screaming, adults were covering their children's eyes, and flashes from cameras were going off all around us. Our picture was still live, and I focused on a body with long blonde hair and absolutely no face, wearing jeans and a flannel shirt, lying in a heap facing my camera.

I heard muffled voices in my ear, then the anchor came on and apologized for what they just showed. They had dropped our picture. The director was livid. He was screaming at us. Scott grabbed the microphone and stood in front of the camera we knew only the control room could see. With a very stern look, he calmly spoke to the director.

"I warned your dumb ass about what could happen," Scott said, "but you knew better, didn't you, you know it all? That's what you get–your viewers heading to bed with visions of a faceless woman dancing in their heads."

We heard silence on the other end. I shut off the camera and unplugged the microphone. Scott put his hand on my shoulder.

"I was running out of shit to say," he said with a smile. "I thought they'd never get that stiff out of that hole. Looks like she had a great body on her."

He laughed and walked away.

# Chapter

 **YOUR NEWS SUCKS**

It was a beautiful, sunny Friday morning. I was coming out of a deli with my morning bagel when the desk called me with something they wanted me to check out. There was a guy threatening to jump off the sixteenth floor of a newly construct-ed building on the near south side of the city. Normally we don't cover suicides, but the commotion this guy was causing was screwing up traffic and causing major congestion in that area.

I parked a few blocks away from the building and had a decent visual on the guy. I could see a man standing out on the ledge, waving his arms and yelling something that none of us at ground level could understand. I zoomed in and got a tight shot of him. He was an older black man. I could see him through the camera lens, talking to the police negotiator.

The longer he stayed there, the larger the group of onlook-ers became. Traffic was getting bad, and people were honking their horns. Some people were even stopping their cars in the middle of the street to get a look at this guy. Eventually, two police officers and their spokesperson made their way through the ever-growing crowd and headed straight for me. The spokesperson put her hand on my shoulder and spoke rather loudly to overcome the crowd noise.

"Can we talk to you?" she asked. "Please come with us."

I broke down my equipment and followed the officers through the police line. I was led to a giant mobile home, which was serving as a portable police headquarters. It was packed with police captains, lieutenants, swat commanders, and one plainclothes officer. Each officer took turns introducing themselves to me. I was really starting to wonder just what I had gotten myself into. The Swat Commander pulled me away from the others and, in a firm but friendly voice, described the situation.

"We can't have this," he said. "It's not good if he jumps. We need your help; will you help us?"

"Sure," I answered. "What can I do?"

A Chicago Police Captain stepped forward. He removed his hat and set it on a table. He cleared his voice and explained.

"The guy up on the scaffolding is someone we've encountered before," he said. "Last year he tried the same shit at the Trump Towers when that was being built. He's bi-polar and suffers from schizophrenia, a fucking ball of fun."

The whole room laughed.

"He claims Oprah Winfrey took an idea he had for a show and used it and never paid him. Since we can't get Oprah to shag her ass up sixteen stories and write him a check, we need to use your camera."

The plain-clothes officer stepped up.

"Last time he did this," he explained, "we got a television crew to come and talk to him. That calmed him down, and he came off the ledge."

"No problem," I replied. "I can do that."

"This time we're thinking I act like you," the plain-clothes officer said. "I'll show him the camera, make him think I'm filming, and then grab him. Less liability."

"One problem," I pointed out. "When you grab him what do you do with the camera? It's a fifty thousand dollar piece of equipment. Break that, and you have a ton of liability."

The Captain turned to the other officers, and everyone was suddenly very quiet.

"How about you act like a reporter and hold the micro-phone," I said, "and I'll be the cameraman. That way, when we get close, all you'll have to drop when you grab him is the microphone."

The officer turned to all his bosses, and they approved. He turned back to me.

"When this happens, just keep your distance," he said.

We walked out of the command center and were greeted by more officers. Their job was to escort us on our sixteen-story journey. We piled into the poorly constructed motorized cage that transported workers as high as thirty stories. There was just a wooden floor and a chain link fence separating us from the ground below, and the cage shook and rattled the entire way up.

We came to a slamming halt and ran down a hallway. The officer and I were escorted into a stairwell that was illuminated by a lone light bulb. Ten members of the Swat team were stand-ing there, equipped with full combat gear, including rifles and handguns, ready for action.

One mentally challenged individual was pitted against enough firepower to take over the city. I stood there, holding a camera next to this group of pissed off heavily armed men who had been there for five hours already. One of the men, a big man with some seriously tattooed arms, inquired why I was there.

"Why are you carrying a camera?" he asked.

The officer with me explained the situation and how they were hoping for a peaceful solution. One of the SWAT team guys snapped.

"Then can anyone tell us why the fuck we've spent the better part of our morning here?" He unsnapped his holster and put his hand on his gun. "Let me shoot this crazy bastard, and we can get lunch."

Everyone laughed. One of the negotiators poked his head around the corner of the darkened stairwell and snapped

"Shut up!" he said. "We're talking to him, he can hear you."

He glared at everyone for a few seconds, before pulling his head back around the corner. The SWAT guys just looked at each other and smiled. Things were quiet except for the occasional shuffling of boots on the metal staircase as each guy jockeyed to find a place to sit. The negotiator walked back into the stairwell and looked right at me.

"Here's the drill," he said. "You two step out about twenty feet. He's going to look at you both. You're playing the reporter," he said to the officer. "Make sure he can see the microphone logo then duck back around the corner. We'll just use you to tease him, at first. Then on your next visit, it will be easier to grab him."

He gave us a nod and left the room again. I turned around to grab my camera off the floor, and one of the SWAT team guys wished me luck.

"Please, bring him in," another one said.

"Tell that asshole to jump please?" another deadpanned.

I nodded back to them all and handed my microphone to the officer. I had this uneasy feeling in my stomach, like something was about to go wrong. What if he grabbed me and took me down with him? What if one of the trigger-happy SWAT guys decided to spray the room with bullets, and I got in the way?

I was second-guessing my decision to be anywhere near this situation. Moments later we got the word that the officer and I should step into clear view of the jumper. He teetered on the edge of a ledge, and the man gave us the once over before turning away. The officers grabbed us and escorted us back into the stairwell.

A few minutes later we heard the "squawking" of a police radio getting closer and closer to us. It was the negotiator, and he was not happy. Motioning for the officer and me to come closer, a call came over his radio.

"Chief, another station said they'd send a camera and a reporter right over, 10-4."

Looking directly at me the negotiator replied back. "10-4."

"What's going on?" I asked.

"I'm sorry," he said in an apologetic tone, "this just isn't working out."

"Wait a minute," I demanded, "What happened? Why did you call another station?"

He stopped and slowly turned around. His eyes scanned the dimly lit stairwell and studied the curious faces.

"He won't talk to you, because your news sucks, all right?"

"What?"

The negotiator was quickly tiring of the whole conversation.

"Look buddy, the jumper said he watches all the news shows, and you guys are the worst. He doesn't want to be on a station no one watches. Thank you for your time."

With that, he walked away. I looked at the officer with me, who handed me back my microphone. He patted me on the shoulder.

"Your news does suck."

I looked over at the SWAT guys who were doing their best not to laugh right in my face. The big tattooed guy piped up.

"How does it feel that a schizophrenic douchebag would rather kill himself than be on your news?"

As we stood by the construction elevator, waiting for it to crawl its way back up the side of the building, my escort spoke to me.

"I heard over the police radio that the jumper wouldn't talk to you because your news sucks."

I nodded. He smiled.

"No offense man, but your news does suck."

When the elevator came to a slamming halt, out hopped a reporter and a cameraman from another station. We exchanged pleasantries as they headed toward the stairwell, when the reporter turned around.

"I heard the guy said your news sucks."

The cameraman and my escort broke into laughter. I got into the elevator, and the door slammed shut. The chain link fence rattled while we hurled downward, down to ground level toward a fair amount of police blue and the spokesperson that had gotten me into this mess. When the door slid open, the spokesperson stepped toward me.

"Good news," she said, "the jumper is in custody."

"That's great," I said through gritted teeth.

She kept walking with me as I was heading out of there.

"Seems the jumper is a big fan of the reporter we sent up

there. The second he saw him he came right off the ledge and into custody."

"Great," I shot back, "Great."

She handed me off to another officer who was to take me to my car. It was a short and heavyset policewoman. Her hat was pulled to the bridge of her nose. We walked past groups of officers, who were all talking amongst themselves as we passed. Smiles and laughter were all around the construction site. My tiny officer friend walked with me all the way to my car. It was a few blocks farther than I'm sure she was required to go. As I put my equipment into the car, she put the icing on my shitty morning cake.

"I watched your station for the longest time," she said, "but now it just doesn't do it for me. The jumper was right; your news sucks. But if makes you feel any better, lately all the news sucks."

\*　\*　\*　\*　\*

## A SNAPSHOT IN TIME/2011/ROD BLAGOJEVICH ON TRIAL

Illinois governor, Rod Blagojevich, was lucky enough to have not one, but two trials. Both trials were long and drawn out. At the second trial, I looked forward to when he and his wife entered the building every morning. Security was tight. All he had to do was walk through a cordoned off area, 50 feet in length, to enter the building. The governor's problem was he could never pass someone without shaking their hand or talking to them. Every day, that 50 foot walk was lined with people who, day after day, felt compelled to wish the fallen politician good luck. It was always entertaining to see his wife forcefully grab his arm and drag him away while he was in mid-conversation with his faithful following. He worked the room like a Vegas lounge singer, and she tried like hell just to keep him in check.

Everyone eventually comes to the point in their lives where they make that decision of what path to take, what instinct to trust, what direction to follow.

God willing, you make your living out of something you have passion for, something that gives you a sense of fulfillment. My uncertain destiny was steadied the second I threw a camera on my shoulder.

It has been an adventure, no two days ever alike. The camera I operate has had a front row seat, chronicling everyday events with the simple depression of a record button. It has recorded people flourishing and struggling, documented things as they unfolded, with no misconceptions and no uncertainty. It tells it as it sees it.

All I've ever known is the inside of a newsroom. I've seen how it's done right, and I count my blessings every night that I had a taste of the way it should be.

They say fewer people are watching television news these days, that today's youth has no interest in current events. As they get older and become consumers, predictions are that television news will be a faint memory. I've heard the naysayers cry, "this is the end" for over thirty years, yet the game goes on. So we struggle to maintain our identity, roll with the technology that comes faster than we can control, and hold the line against the lack of ideals that are taking our business in a downward direction.

When I look back at the years of doing something I honestly loved, it's been the people I've stood shoulder to shoulder with on a daily basis that made this lifelong journey truly satisfying.

No complaints here.

It's been a great Life Behind The Camera.

# ACKNOWLEDGEMENTS

I would first and foremost like to thank Rick Kaempfer and David Stern. Thank you gentlemen for giving me the opportunity to fulfill a long time goal of publishing a book. You took a chance on me and I cannot thank you guys enough.

To my designer, Vasil Nazar for the great cover and interior design and my editor, Ashley McDonald for helping me polish the text.

To Joan Hastings, you were the first person to help with the book in the early stages and I thank you for your support and encouragement.

To Paul Nagaro, Jim Stricklin, and Dave Durham for your friendship and guidance in my NBC years and beyond.

To Lisa Vucsko, Patrick Elwood, Darlene Hill, Dane Placko, Steve Erwin, Joe and Glinda LoVerde and others too many to mention, thank you for your advice and never ending encouragement.

To my parents Pete and Nancy, thank you for always being there and giving me a life time of love and support.

To my brother Mike, a life long Cub fan and despite that devastating flaw, my best friend.

To my children, Caitlin, Andrew, and Elizabeth, you guys are everything and more a father could hope for.

To my wife Nancy, it's been an incredible journey through life so far, and I'm honored that you've been by my side. Love you.

# ABOUT THE AUTHOR

 **CHUCK QUINZIO** has worked as a television cameraman in Chicago for thirty years. During that time he has seen and filmed it all. "Life Behind the Camera" is a memoir that recounts some truly amazing tales; some tragic, some historic, and some that are just plain laugh out loud funny. This is his first book, and will be released via Eckhartz Press in Fall 2013.

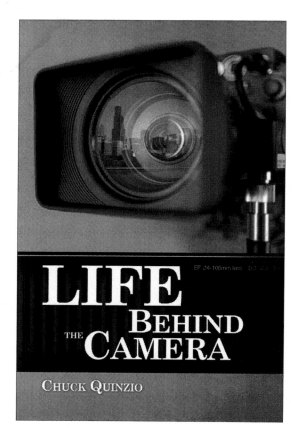

LIFE BEHIND THE CAMERA is available at:

## www.EckhartzPress.com

ECKHARTZ
PRESS